West Academic Publishing's Law School Advisory Board

a short & happy guide to

Appellate Advocacy

Rodd W. Barckhoff

A SHORT & HAPPY GUIDE® SERIES

WEST ACADEMIC

860 Blue Gentian Road, Suite 350
Eagan, MN 55121
1-877-888-1330

Published in the United States of America

ISBN: 979-8-89209-720-8

Acknowledgments

This book contains much of what I've learned about legal writing and appellate advocacy over the past three decades. But it's far from all there is to know. There are many great resources and voices of authority on the topics of legal analysis and legal writing. Be open to different methods and find what works for you. Be willing to ask questions and seek help. Speaking of which, I need to thank everyone who helped or inspired me to write this guide.

- Kailyn R. Stone, a 2025 graduate of the University of Tennessee Winston College of Law. In addition to finishing with highest honors and serving as Editor-In-Chief of the *Tennessee Law Review*, Kailyn found time to review, research, and organize these materials. More importantly, she assured me that the book is "funny" and that students "probably won't even mind reading it." That's high praise.
- Colleagues at the University of Tennessee Winston College of Law, especially:
    - Paula Schaeffer, Art Stolnitz Distinguished Professor, who reviewed initial drafts and offered her knowledge, support, and great friendship;
    - Professor Emerita Penny White for her wisdom, inspiration, and friendship; and former Professor and Director of Legal Writing Carol Parker for giving me an opportunity to teach and then showing me how.
- Everyone at West Academic.
- My two (grown) children, John and Mary, and my entire family. My mom, Judy Mellinger, even

reviewed some rough drafts, just like she did when I was in high school. Thanks, Mom!

- My wonderful wife, Christine, edited countless rough drafts, made valuable suggestions, and laughed out loud in all the right places. More importantly, she never stopped believing I had something to offer. "Thank-you" is not saying nearly enough.

And finally, this guide is dedicated to the hundreds of students (Barckhoff alums) I've met along the way. (You know who you are.) You gave me more than you know and far more than I can express. The opportunity to have played some small role in your legal journey was an honor and privilege.

Table of Contents

PART FOUR. REVISIONS

A Short & Happy Guide to Appellate Advocacy

Introduction

Welcome to the *Short and Happy Guide to Appellate Advocacy!* As someone who has practiced and taught appellate litigation for over thirty years, I'm pleased that the materials in this guide have found a short and happy home. And a little surprised.

One word rarely used to describe the appellate process is "short." And a feeling rarely associated with appellate brief writing is "happy." In fact, prior versions of this material had these working titles:

- *Winning on Appeal: Good Luck with That.*
- *Appellate Advocacy: Running the Gauntlet.*
- *If I'd Had More Time, the Brief Would Have Been Shorter.*
- *Dead Bodies, Word Gravel, and Legal Writing.*

Let's just say that if you enjoy a challenge, you're in the right place. How much of a challenge? Take a deep breath and repeat after me:

"Affirmed."

Congratulations. Without knowing a single detail, you just correctly predicted the outcome in over 90 percent of all appeals. One study revealed that federal appellate courts had an overall affirmance rate of nearly 92 percent over a 12-month period.[1] The odds of a reversal in criminal appeals? Roughly 6 percent.[2] Yikes. Not surprisingly, there's a name for this: affirmation bias.[3] And if you're wondering, appellants do not fare much better in state appeals.[4]

At this point, you may be thinking, "Hey, I was told there'd be no math."

Behind these grim statistics are people who may have to pay damages, go to jail, deal with a catastrophic injury, lose custody of their children, or handle any number of other adverse rulings. They may be angry, frightened, and frustrated. They may be confused about complex issues and unfamiliar with tedious procedures. They will want your immediate expert advice about the next steps in the proceedings.

And by that, I mean they will look at you and say, "Now what?"

The good news is there are *a lot* of excellent books and articles about legal writing and appellate advocacy, and each one is filled with hundreds of suggestions, techniques, and examples. There are also online resources, websites, tutorials, videos, and yes, even a

---

[1] *See Table B-5. U.S. Courts of Appeals—Decisions in Cases Terminated on the Merits, by Circuit and Nature of Proceeding, During the 12-Month Period Ending September 30, 2024*, https://www.uscourts.gov/sites/default/files/2024-12/jb_b5_0930.2024.pdf.

[2] Barry C. Edwards, *Why Appeals Courts Rarely Reverse Lower Courts: An Experimental Study to Explore Affirmation Bias*, 68 Emory L.J. Online 1035, 1037 (2019).

[3] *See id.* at 1043 ("Affirmation bias in an appellate case is the tendency to affirm a prior decision for reasons unrelated to the relative merits of the parties' arguments or the applicable standard of review.").

[4] *Id.* at 1039 ("State appellate courts reverse lower courts at similarly low rates [as federal courts].)."

few podcasts. In recent years, artificial intelligence has created new opportunities—and risks.

The bad news is that students and young lawyers can get overwhelmed or lost. Some struggle to get words on the page. Others adopt a "more is more" approach and hope for the best. And a great many produce a brief at the last minute with no real approach or semblance of a plan.

The *Short and Happy Guide to Appellate Advocacy* will make sure that doesn't happen to you. Intended for young lawyers and students who have had at least one semester of legal writing and analysis, this guide covers several key areas.

- Part one talks about preserving issues, executing appeals, and avoiding procedural pitfalls such as waiver. Want some more math? Without viable issues to raise, the odds of prevailing on appeal are exactly zero.
- Part two discusses the importance of making a great first impression with an appellate brief. This includes the technical components of the brief, the Statement of Facts, and the Statement of Issues. The goal is to engage readers even before they get to your legal analysis and arguments.
- Part three covers the most demanding aspect of appellate advocacy: developing persuasive arguments. We will discuss basic legal analysis and structural devices like CREAC. And we will delve into methods for showing the court *what* result to reach, *how* to reach that result, and *why* to reach that result.
- Finally, part four turns rough drafts into polished briefs. There is an old saying: "Don't mistake activity

> for achievement." And there's another old saying: "Don't mistake the longest brief for the best brief." The best brief is the one that is organized, clear, and accurate.

Each part of the guide features hundreds of engaging examples written by law students, along with my comments as teaching moments. The examples illustrate traditional and alternative methods while also showing there is more than one way to accomplish any given task.

Will we cover every nuance of legal writing and analytical pedagogy? No. After all, we want this *Short and Happy* guide to be relatively short and reasonably happy. But we will cover the skills a successful appellate advocate must have. And we will lay the groundwork for continued improvement throughout your education and career.

As I said earlier, if you love a challenge, this unique and demanding area of practice is for you. The numbers and odds show us that. This guide will teach you to identify issues, execute appeals, write persuasive briefs, and represent clients with competence and diligence. That's good. With time, dedication, and experience, this guide will help you develop your own voice and a reputation for excellence. And that's great.

Although the challenges remain, success will follow. Let's get started!

PART ONE

Hope to Win, Prepare to Appeal

CHAPTER I

Preserving Issues

Before getting into appellate *advocacy*, let's discuss appellate *procedure*. An advocate's grasp of the entire appellate process may be the single most important part of appellate advocacy.[1] More important than legal acumen. More important than eloquent writing and rhetoric. And *way* more important than the Bluebook.

Appellate procedure is an extremely detailed topic. On the federal level, we have a supreme court, thirteen circuit courts of appeal, and nearly 100 district courts.[2] Other federal courts involve specialized areas like tax, bankruptcy, administrative law, veterans' affairs, and more.

We also have fifty state courts of last resort (often, but not always, called the supreme court) and at least fifty state intermediate appellate courts. Some states have several intermediate appellate court divisions, and others have appellate

---

1 The title for part one of this guide—Hope to Win, Prepare to Appeal—is the philosophy expressed by legendary Tennessee lawyer Jerry Summers. *See* Jerry H. Summers, *Hope to Win, Prepare to Appeal* (2022). Mr. Summers is one of the key founders of the Center for Advocacy and Dispute Resolution at the University of Tennessee Winston College of Law.

2 *Introduction to the Federal Court System*, Off. of the U.S. Attorneys, https://www.justice.gov/usao/justice-101/federal-courts (last visited Aug. 30, 2024).

courts for criminal cases. Every jurisdiction has hundreds of procedural rules and internal rules.

In the interest of being *Short and Happy,* this guide will narrow the scope by referring to supreme courts, appellate courts, and trial courts. Although we will discuss the federal rules of procedure for illustration, the rules in each jurisdiction may differ. The good news is appellate process is something you need to *know,* but it's not something you need to *memorize.* In fact, you're generally better off if you don't even try to memorize. Just look things up. If you know how the appellate process works, you will know what to look for in any jurisdiction.

A. Waiver

Lesson one. Any chance for success on appeal is tied to what happens from the very first day a lawyer meets with a client. A lawyer's professional duties include competence and diligence. That means investigating the facts, conducting research, and raising claims, defenses, and issues as early as possible.[3] That also means filing pretrial motions, making objections and offers of proof at trial, and executing appeals. Put simply, a lawyer's failure to do these things properly and timely means that issues and objections may not be reviewed on appeal if the case is later lost.

There's a word for this: waiver.

In over 87 percent of appeals, at least one issue is deemed waived by an appellate court. Okay, I just made up that statistic, but the actual percentage is probably even higher. Sure, you may still raise unpreserved issues, but you'll face the extremely difficult task of showing plain error, as we'll talk about later. By "extremely difficult," I mean "next to impossible."

---

3 *See* MODEL RULES OF PRO. CONDUCT r. 1.1, 1.3 (AM. BAR ASS'N 1983).

Remember the clients who were unhappy, frightened, and confused about losing? They won't feel any better when they learn their appeal hasn't been considered on the merits because the issues were waived. I can tell you that losing on the merits is far better because you can simply tell the client the court was wrong and it's not your fault. But the *Short and Happy Guide to Losing on the Merits* doesn't sound inspiring.

The news is not all bad. If you are the appellee, feel free to tell the court that the *other* side failed to file a pretrial motion, failed to object at trial, failed to make an offer of proof, failed to file post-judgment motions, failed to properly execute the appeal, and so on. In other words, even if you plan to be that rare attorney who wins every case at trial (and you know who you are), this guide will still be useful. So, you're welcome.

B. Identifying and Raising Issues

We need to begin with a little bit of civil procedure, criminal procedure, pretrial litigation, discovery, and trial practice. Remember we are looking at broad concepts, not specific procedures. And the details may vary in each jurisdiction.

1. Pleadings

Pleadings include things like complaints, counterclaims, third-party complaints, and answers.[4] They must contain claims and defenses that have evidentiary support.[5] That requires competent and diligent investigations. They must also be "warranted by existing law or by a nonfrivolous argument for extending, modifying,

[4] Fed. R. Civ. P. 7(a); *see* Fed. R. Civ. P. 12(b) ("Every defense to a claim for relief in any pleading must be asserted in the responsive pleading if one is required.").

[5] Fed. R. Civ. P. 11.

or reversing existing law or for establishing new law."[6] That requires competent and diligent research.

What does all this mean?

If claims and defenses are not asserted at the very beginning, don't even think about mentioning them on appeal. I once read an appellate brief in a property dispute in which a lawyer asked the appellate court to award damages because his client had been defamed by the opposing party. The only problem was the lawyer did not assert a claim for defamation in the complaint. Granted, boundary disputes between feuding neighbors can get heated and there's no telling who might be called what. But raising a claim for defamation for the first time in an appellate brief? Not a good idea. I could tell you the judges simply laughed in the lawyer's general direction. But that would suggest they were amused. They weren't.

I suppose this is a good time to mention that a lawyer's failure to properly raise claims, assert defenses, and preserve issues does not only affect appeals. They can also result in a client's claim of legal malpractice in civil cases or ineffective assistance of counsel in criminal cases.

And there's nothing short or happy about those topics.

2. *Motions*

In addition to pleadings, some matters may be brought to the trial court's attention by motion. In federal *civil* cases,[7] for example, these include: (1) lack of subject-matter jurisdiction; (2) lack of personal jurisdiction; (3) improper venue; (4) insufficient process; (5) insufficient service of process; (6) failure to state a claim upon which relief can be granted; and (7) failure to join a party under Rule 19. If you have grounds to support these issues,

---

6 *Id.*; *see also* MODEL RULES OF PRO. CONDUCT r. 1.1, 1.3 (AM. BAR ASS'N 1983).

7 Fed. R. Civ. P. 12(b).

raise them before trial (or else risk, well, think of a word that starts with "w" and ends with "aiver").

In federal *criminal* cases,[8] a motion challenging jurisdiction may be made at any time. All other motions *must* be made before trial. The list covers *a lot* of ground:

- motions alleging a defect in instituting the prosecution (venue, delay, speedy trial, grand-jury proceedings);
- motions alleging a defect in the charging instrument (duplicity, multiplicity, specificity, joinder, failure to state an offense);
- motions to suppress evidence;
- motions to sever the charges or defendants; and
- motions for discovery.

Could I invent some percentage of cases in which issues were waived because they were not raised in a pretrial motion? Yes, and I'm tempted. But would the actual percentage likely be higher? Also, yes.

Matters may also be raised before trial by filing motions in limine. These are motions that ask the trial court for a pretrial ruling about the admissibility of evidence or argument.[9] They generally are not mandatory, but they are important matters of tactics and strategy. When the trial court resolves a matter before trial, the parties can prepare without suspense, surprise, or the risk of waiver.

In short, success on appeal is tied to a lawyer's ability to identify and raise claims and issues before trial. That takes competent and diligent representation from day one. Therefore,

---

[8] Fed. R. Crim. P. 12(b)(2).

[9] *Black's Law Dictionary* 526 (5th ed. 1983).

even if you only represent the client on appeal, you'd better hope the trial lawyers did a good job.

3. *Objections and Offers of Proof*

Not everything can be raised before trial. Many issues involving evidence, misconduct, and jury instructions arise *during trial.* When they do, a trial lawyer must be ready to object. And when they relate to evidentiary issues, Rule 103(a)(1) of the Federal Rules of Evidence has this to say:

> (a) Preserving a Claim of Error. A party may claim error in a ruling to admit or exclude evidence *only if* the error affects a *substantial right* of the party and:
>
> > (1) if the ruling admits evidence, a party, on the record:
> >
> > > (A) *timely objects or moves to strike*; and
> > >
> > > (B) *states the specific ground*, unless it was apparent from the context. . . .

(Emphasis added because this cannot be overemphasized).

A *timely* objection means "contemporaneous." That means if trial lawyers fail to object when a possible error occurs, an appellate court may decide they failed to take action to avoid any harm. A *specific* objection means exactly that. Lawyers must identify the proper basis for their objections. Otherwise, you know what might happen if those issues are raised on appeal. (Ahem, waiver, cough, ahem.)

But wait, there's more.

If the trial court's ruling *excludes* evidence, the proponent of the evidence must "inform[ ] the court of its substance by an offer of proof, unless the substance was apparent from the context."[10] Why? Because the appellate court cannot review what's not in the record. Wait, that's a double negative. The appellate court can only review what's in the record. That's better. If an offer of proof is not made, the appellate court will presume the trial court's ruling was correct. Hmmm, what's another way to say that? The appellant will lose.[11]

So, what's the message to students who want to be trial lawyers and trial lawyers who claim they don't do appellate work?

Rule 103, that's the message.

4. Post-Trial Proceedings

Competence and diligence extend to post-judgment matters as well. In fact, there are a lot of things to think about.

a. Preparing the Client

The practice of law is filled with risk. Whenever a court is likely to rule on a dispositive motion or the trier of fact is ready to deliver a verdict, lawyers should discuss the possible scenarios with their clients in advance. Clients may not understand the appellate process or the difference between a jury trial and appellate review. They may not know whether a judgment may be stayed or whether they may be taken into custody after a guilty verdict. Although it may not completely soften the emotional blow of an adverse ruling, preparing will go a long way in communicating with clients and protecting their interests.

b. Scope of Representation

Speaking of protecting the client's interests, lawyers cannot simply disappear after an adverse ruling or verdict (regardless of

---

[10] Fed. R. Evid. 103(a)(2).

[11] *Id.*

how much they want to). Even lawyers who intend to withdraw and hand the case to some appellate lawyer must make sure clients know and understand that arrangement well in advance. The scope of representation should be clarified in writing with the rest of an initial agreement with a client. That will reduce the chance that failures or mistakes in the post-judgment proceedings affect the client's chances on appeal.

c. Post-Trial Motions

Post-trial motions allow a trial judge to correct any errors or grant any necessary relief before an appeal is taken. They include things like motions for judgment as a matter of law, motions for a new trial, motions for judgment notwithstanding the verdict, motions to alter or amend the judgment, and others.[12]

The first thing to remember is that post-trial motions must be filed within a certain number of days after the court enters a judgment. Here's one good example of why you must always check the rules: a motion for a new trial must be filed within 28 days of the entry of judgment in a civil case but within 14 days of a verdict or finding of guilt in a criminal case.[13] The simple reason for that difference is, well, actually, I have no idea.

The second thing to remember is that even though most post-trial motions are denied (oops, spoiler alert), they are tied to the appeal. For example, some jurisdictions require a timely motion for a new trial to preserve appellate review of the issues listed in the

---

[12] *See* Fed. R. Civ. P. 50, 52, 59(a), 59(e); *see also* Fed. R. Crim. P. 33.

[13] Fed. R. Civ. P. 59 ("A motion for a new trial must be filed no later than 28 days after the entry of judgment."); Fed. R. Crim. P. 33(b)(2) ("Other Grounds. Any motion for a new trial grounded on any reason other than newly discovered evidence must be filed within 14 days after the verdict or finding of guilty.").

motion.[14] And some appellate courts will review only those issues that are specifically stated in the motion.[15]

Post-trial matters can be complex so always double and triple check the rules. For instance, a judgment as a matter of law must be made during a federal trial to renew it post-trial; an appellate court can then review the sufficiency of the evidence.[16] But federal appellate courts do not require that an issue be raised in a motion for a new trial if an objection was made at trial.[17]

Here's something to consider. In some jurisdictions, an issue that was raised before and during trial may *still be* considered waived unless specifically raised in a timely motion for a new trial. If you are wondering, this does *not* always work the other way. A failure to raise an issue before trial or object during trial may *not* be forgiven by including that issue in a motion for a new trial. Have fun explaining all *that* to a client.

In short, the details are often complex, but the message is clear. Post-trial motions are tied directly to the appeal. The safest approach may be to file pretrial motions, trial objections, and post-trial motions. Raise and renew issues early and often. I mean, why take chances? Think of it as wearing a belt and suspenders at the same time. (Or don't, because that's a pretty silly image.)

---

[14] *See* Tenn. R. App. P. 3(e) (explaining that an appellate court may dismiss the appeal if the appellant does not timely file a notice of appeal).

[15] *Id.*

[16] *Unitherm Food Systems v. Swith-Eckrich, Inc.*, 546 US 394 (2006).

[17] 11 Wright, et al., *Federal Practice and Procedure* § 2818 (2d ed.1995) ("settled rule in federal courts . . . is that a party may assert on appeal any question that has been properly raised in the trial court. Parties are not required to make a motion for a new trial challenging the supposed errors as a prerequisite to appeal.")

And One More Thing

Let's end this chapter where we began: Hope to win, prepare to appeal. That begins from day one.

CHAPTER II

Executing Appeals

Executing an appeal means knowing where to go and how to get there. Although appeals can go by a variety of names, the most common are appeals as of right, interlocutory appeals, and appeals by permission.

A. Appeal as of Right

1. Final Judgment

The first requirement for pursuing an appeal as of right is the trial court's entry of a final judgment. A final judgment is one that "adjudicat[es] all of the claims and all the parties' rights and liabilities."[1] That can be trickier than it sounds in complex cases involving multiple parties and multiple claims. The end of a case for one party may be the middle of the case for others. Therefore, the district court may enter a partial final judgment regarding an issue

1 Fed. R. Civ. P. 54(b).

or a party.[2] For our purposes, a final judgment means the trial court has disposed of the entire case and has nothing left to do.[3]

2. *Notice of Appeal*

When a final judgment is filed, the clock starts for a party to execute an appeal by filing a notice of appeal. A notice of appeal contains the case style, the docket number, the name of the appealing party, the date of the final judgment, and the court to which the appeal is taken.[4] Once the notice is properly filed and served on the other parties, everyone knows an appeal is underway.[5]

Although the notice of appeal form is simple, the details may vary. In federal court, the notice of appeal must be filed with the clerk of the trial court.[6] In other jurisdictions, the notice must be filed with the clerk of the appellate court.

The time for filing a notice of appeal may also vary. Under the federal rules, the time depends on the type of case and the party who executes the appeal.[7] For example, the defendant in a criminal case has 14 days from the entry of the judgment being appealed in which to file a notice of appeal; the government has 30 days. A party in a federal civil case has 30 days from the entry of the judgment being appealed to file a notice of appeal; but if a United States agency, employee, or officer is involved, parties have 60 days in which to file a notice of appeal. Don't bother memorizing these time

---

[2] *Id.*

[3] By the way, in criminal cases this can include final judgments that are the product of guilty pleas. For example, a defendant who pleads guilty may often appeal the sentence. *See* Fed. R. Crim. P. 32(j)(1)(B). Or a defendant may enter a conditional guilty plea while reserving the right to appeal the trial court's ruling on a pretrial motion. Fed. R. Crim. P. 11(a)(2). For our purposes, we will just consider these final judgments.

[4] Fed. R. App. P. 3(c)(1).

[5] *Id.* at 3(d).

[6] *Id.* at 3(a)(1).

[7] *Id.* at 4(a), 4(b).

periods; for all we know, they may have changed from the time I wrote this passage. Always look at the rules.

There are other considerations. The filing of some post-trial motions—such as a motion for new trial—may stop the clock for filing a notice of appeal. When the trial court rules on the post-trial motion, the time for filing a notice of appeal starts from the entry of *that* order. Make sense?[8] As you can see, post-judgment proceedings can get detailed and tricky. And there can be serious consequences for any missteps. Under the federal rules, for example, the time for filing a notice of appeal can be extended but a lawyer must show excusable neglect or good cause.[9] In other jurisdictions, the failure to file a timely notice of appeal may result in the dismissal of the appeal. Which, in turn, may result in a client googling "legal malpractice."

3. Record on Appeal

a. What Is It?

In most jurisdictions, a timely notice of appeal starts a period in which the appellant must designate, order, and file a record on appeal. The record on appeal includes the pleadings, motions, trial transcripts, post-trial motions, orders, and judgments that are relevant to the issues raised on appeal.[10] Although most records are now filed electronically, you might think of the record as a big box of stuff. Anything that happened before, during, or after the trial goes into that box. And then that box is shipped to the judges on the court of appeals. (In fact, it's often still done that way in many jurisdictions).

---

8 *Id.* at 4(a)(4)(i-vi); 4(b)(3)(i)-(iii).

9 *Id.* at 4(a)(5); 4(b)(4).

10 *Id.* at 10(a)(1).

Under the federal rules, the appellant has 14 days to file the record with the trial court clerk.[11] In some cases, less than the entire record will suffice.[12] But if the appellant orders less than the entire record, the appellee may designate additional portions to include.[13] After the record is filed, the trial court clerk is required to assemble the material and forward it to the circuit court clerk.[14] A separate appendix is also filed that contains the relevant material from the record.[15] The appeal is then docketed in the appellate court.

b. Why Is This Important?

Because the appellate court has no idea what happened in your case, other than what it finds in that box (or the electronic version of that box). If something is missing from that box, the appellate court will have no choice but to presume the trial court's ruling was correct. What's another way to put that? Oh, yes. The appellant will lose.

This may make more sense when viewed with some practical scenarios.

- If you plan to argue that the trial court erred in denying a motion to suppress your client's statement under the 5th and 14th amendments, the record on appeal needs to contain the motion to suppress, a copy of the client's statement, the transcript of any relevant pretrial hearings, the transcript of the trial, and the trial court's ruling.

---

[11] *Id.* at 10(a), (b).

[12] *Id.* at 10(b)(3).

[13] *Id.*

[14] *Id.* at 11.

[15] *Id.* at 30.

- If you are challenging the trial court's ruling that your expert witness was not qualified to testify, the record needs to contain your motion, any evidence showing the expert's qualifications, the transcript of any relevant pretrial hearings, an offer of proof showing what the expert would have said at trial, the trial transcript, and the trial court's ruling.
- Challenging the qualifications of a juror? The record needs the jury selection transcript, your objection, and the trial court's ruling.
- Challenging the opposing side's closing argument? The record needs the transcript of the closing argument, your objection, the transcript of the trial, and the court's ruling.
- Arguing that a document was admissible? That document needs to be in the record, along with the trial court's ruling.
- Did you argue that an exhibit was inadmissible? Well, you know the rest.

c. The Risk of Waiver (Yet Again)

Here's the bottom line: an issue that was raised before, during, and after the trial may be considered waived by the appellate court if something is omitted from the record. If this sounds technical, you won't be shocked to learn that many of us of a certain age often refer to the record on appeal as "the technical record." So, you might think of these as technicalities.

(Thank you, I'll show myself out).

Good news.

Attorneys who understand the importance of the appellate record have an advantage. If something has been inadvertently omitted from the record, a lawyer can file a written motion asking either the trial court or the appellate court to supplement the record.[16] As we will see in the next section, an appellate motion simply requires you to show that an item is missing from the record that should have been included—a transcript, a motion, an exhibit—and ask the court for an order allowing the material to be included. Point out that the material is needed for effective review of the appeal.

But.

This does *not* mean adding things to the record that were not introduced during the proceedings in the trial court.[17] Oops, that was a double negative again. You can only supplement the record with material that was considered in the trial court. You can't add any material—a witness statement, document, photograph, or anything else—unless it was considered by the trial judge.

4. *Appellate Motions*

After an appeal is docketed in the appellate court, additional matters may be raised by motion. As noted above, one common motion asks to supplement or correct the record. Other motions ask the court to grant additional time for the filing of the notice of appeal, the record, the brief, and so on.

Like any motion, an appellate motion requires a written request for relief. The motion should include the parties, the docket number, a description of the case, and a precise statement of the relief that's sought. The motion should be accompanied by an affidavit containing factual assertions in support of the motion.[18] Submitting a proposed order for the court's review is also a good

---

16 *Id.* at 10(e).

17 *Id.*

18 *Id.*

idea and is often required. In addition, here are a few practical things to keep in mind when filing motions.

First, always try to file a motion *before* any existing deadline has expired. That shows the court you haven't let anything fall through the cracks. If you miss a deadline, then you may need to file a motion asking for permission to file a late motion, and no one wants to get in the habit of doing that.

Second, make sure you have a solid reason for the request, particularly when asking for an extension or other relief from a deadline. That doesn't mean you have to be trapped in a well or bleeding from your ears. But it does mean a physical illness or an unavoidable scheduling conflict. And it generally does not mean a computer glitch, a vacation, a momentary lapse of reasoning, or an unspecified workload.

Third, ask the opposing party to agree to the motion or, at least, to agree not to object to the motion. This may be required by court rule, but is a good idea regardless.

Finally, if a motion is filed because an administrative error or mistake was made, never shift the blame to an assistant, a court clerk, the postal service, the barista who got your order wrong, or anyone else. Just accept responsibility and ask the court not to hold your error against your client.

5. Stays and Appeal Bonds

Because executing an appeal may take a few weeks to a few months, make sure the client doesn't suffer harm or prejudice in the meantime. How? Good question that I just asked.

In a civil case, a motion to stay the enforcement of the judgment or other order pending the appeal may be needed. The stay may be conditioned on the filing of a bond or other security. In such cases, the motion must be filed in the trial court; if relief is denied, a motion for review may be pursued in the appellate court.[19] The motion for review should be accompanied by the trial court's ruling on the motion to stay, an affidavit containing any factual allegations, and any parts of the record needed for the appellate court's review.

In a criminal case, a motion to stay may be needed after a conviction so that a defendant can avoid serving the sentence while pursuing the appeal.[20] Again, the motion must be filed in the trial court. And it will likely require a showing that the defendant is not a danger to others and does not pose a risk of flight.[21] (Put another way, don't expect to get a lot of appeal bonds in cases involving convictions for homicide, aggravated assault, sexual offenses, escape, and other serious felonies). The trial court may grant a stay while requiring the defendant to post bond and comply with numerous other conditions. But if the trial court denies a stay, a motion for review may be filed in the appellate court. The motion for review should include the trial court's order, the judgment of conviction, and any other parts of the record needed to determine whether a stay is appropriate.[22]

The important thing is to recognize the options and pursue them. Make sure an appeal is not adversely affected before it's heard.

6. *Briefs and Oral Argument*

After the record on appeal has been filed with the appellate court clerk, the case is docketed and—at long last—it's time to work

---

[19] *Id.* at 8; Fed. R. Civ. P. 62.

[20] *Id.* at 9; Fed. R. Crim. P. 38.

[21] *See* 18 U.S.C. § 3143.

[22] Fed. R. App. P. 9.

on the briefs.[23] Good news. Most of the rest of this guide is devoted to working on the briefs.

In a federal appeal, the appellant has forty days to file a brief after the appeal is docketed. The appellee has thirty days from the filing of the appellant's brief. And the appellant gets the last word by filing a reply brief within twenty-one days of the appellee's brief.[24] These time periods vary, so always check the rules.

As noted earlier, it's not uncommon to file a motion asking for additional time in which to file the brief. Be sure to ask *before* the applicable period expires. Have a good reason for the request. Try not to blame anyone else. And try not to ask for more than one extension.

After the briefs are filed, the case may be set for oral argument before the appellate court. More on those later.

B. Interlocutory Appeals

Although the entry of a final judgment is required for initiating an appeal as of right, you often need to consider an appeal *before* a final judgment is entered. These are called interlocutory appeals. For example, an interlocutory appeal is available whenever a federal court grants, denies, modifies, or dissolves injunctive relief.[25] Similarly, the so-called collateral order doctrine permits interlocutory review to review an important issue that would be "effectively unreviewable" on appeal from a final judgment.[26]

In most cases, though, an interlocutory appeal requires *permission* from both the trial court *and* the appellate court. You read that correctly. A party who seeks interlocutory review of a trial

---

23 *Id.* at 10, 11, 12.

24 *Id.* at 31.

25 28 U.S.C. § 1292(a).

26 *Coopers & Lybrand v. Livesay*, 437 U.S. 463, 468 (1978).

judge's ruling must first file a written motion asking that same trial judge for permission to seek review of that same ruling. It's a little like saying, "We'd like to see the manager."

In most cases, the request filed with the trial court often combines the form of a motion with that of an appellate brief. For example, the components usually include the case names, docket numbers, nature of the case, summary of facts, and statement of the issue or issues.

The written request must also contain your arguments for why review is necessary. That means more than arguing the merits of the issue. That means convincing the court that the issue "involves a controlling question of law as to which there is substantial ground for difference of opinion,"[27] and that "an immediate appeal from the order may materially advance the ultimate termination of the litigation."[28] In other words, an interlocutory appeal makes sense before going any further and risking that an error requires a do-over of the entire proceedings.

As noted above, if the trial court makes the required findings and grants permission for an interlocutory appeal, the party seeking review must then ask the appropriate appellate court for permission to appeal.[29] The written request with the appellate court is similar to the motion filed in the trial court but with a bit more content. For example, remember that the appellate court has no idea of what is happening with your case in the trial court. So, the request for an interlocutory appeal in the appellate court must include the trial court's orders and any relevant material from the record—documents, transcripts, exhibits, etc. That way the appellate court will have something to review. If the appellate court agrees that an appeal is appropriate, the interlocutory appeal can proceed.

---

[27] *Id.* § 1292(b); Fed. R. App. P. 5.

[28] 28 U.S.C. § 1292(b).

[29] *Id.*

What does this all mean in practice?

1. *Choose Wisely*

In most cases, the trial court's ruling on a pretrial motion or objection at trial will *not* meet the criteria for an interlocutory appeal. You will be the subject of a lot of eyerolling (or worse) if you seek interlocutory review of every ruling. Here are some rulings that generally will *not* merit interlocutory review:

- A trial court's decisions regarding the scheduling of discovery, hearings, trial, and other matters. These are largely discretionary issues.
- A trial court's rulings on evidentiary matters such as relevance and hearsay. If the case goes to trial, the losing party may seek review of those rulings on direct appeal.
- A trial court's ruling on a defendant's motion to suppress evidence. That can be reviewed on direct appeal if the defendant is convicted.

Just to clarify, you may disagree with the trial court's rulings and plan to challenge those rulings after a final judgment. But here we are talking about whether to seek *interlocutory* review before a final judgment. Consider an interlocutory appeal only when you have a good faith basis about the following:

- The trial court's ruling involves a controlling question of law.
- Other courts have reached different conclusions on that question of law.
- Resolving the question of law will possibly shorten or even resolve the proceedings.
- Review after a final judgment will be ineffective.

Here are some examples where interlocutory review *might* be requested.

- The trial court's ruling on whether a cause of action exists under a recently enacted statute as a matter of law. If courts have reached different results on that question, an interlocutory appeal may be a good idea.
- The trial court's ruling on a question of law in a case that is complex, involves a lot of witnesses, and will take several weeks to try.
- A trial court's ruling on whether a defendant must submit to a mental health evaluation before a capital murder trial. It's likely a good idea to get that straightened out before going to trial.
- A trial court's denial of a motion to dismiss based on double jeopardy grounds. One purpose of double jeopardy is to avoid subjecting someone to a trial; that purpose could not be achieved if the motion is denied, and the person is tried.

To get a better idea of how to proceed, it's always a good idea to research the cases in which interlocutory review has been granted. That may give you more insight into your options. Otherwise, exercise restraint when asking for interlocutory review.

2. Address the Reasons for Immediate Review

Although the merits of your argument are obviously important, make sure a request for interlocutory review addresses the criteria for granting review. As suggested above, the factors usually include the following:

- Does the issue present a question of law.

- Have courts disagreed or taken different approaches in similar cases.
- Do the issues arise in a complex case or a case that will take a relatively long time to resolve.
- Is there an inherent urgency to the case, such as a capital case or an elections matter.

In short, you will get to argue the merits if the interlocutory appeal is granted. But make sure you get that opportunity.[30] Oh, and if you *do* get that opportunity, remember to file a motion asking the trial court to stay the proceedings to preserve the status quo.[31] That doesn't always happen automatically. The appeal will then proceed like any other: a record on appeal is prepared and filed, the appeal is docketed, both parties file briefs, and the court hears oral arguments. The appellate court's decision on the merits will dictate what happens from there.

C. Appeal by Permission

Whether it's an appeal as of right or an interlocutory appeal, will you be shocked when the appellate court affirms the trial court's judgment? No. That's what they do 90 percent of the time. But you're not out of options.

You can ask the United States Supreme Court or a state's highest court to consider your appeal. But there's a catch. You must

[30] One more note. Interlocutory appeals are either allowed in certain cases or otherwise dependent on the trial court's finding that review is appropriate. But what if the trial court says no? Many jurisdictions have procedures that allow the appellate court to grant a request for interlocutory review even if the trial court denied the request. In federal court, for example, the All Writs Act—while procedurally is considered an original action—allows a party to seek review in rare instance when there is no other avenue of appellate review. *See* 28 U.S.C. § 1651.

[31] Fed. R. App. P. 8; Fed. R. Crim. P. 38.

ask and the answer is nearly always no.[32] These numbers are from the United States Supreme Court's website:

> The Term of the Court begins, by law, on the first Monday in October and lasts until the first Monday in October of the next year. Each Term, approximately 5,000-7,000 new cases are filed in the Supreme Court. This is a substantially larger volume of cases than was presented to the Court in the last century. In the 1950 Term, for example, the Court received only 1,195 new cases, and even as recently as the 1975 Term it received only 3,940. Plenary review, with oral arguments by attorneys, is currently granted in about 80 of those cases each Term, and the Court typically disposes of about 100 or more cases without plenary review.

That's 80 cases out of 5000. That's roughly 1.6 percent. In fairness, the numbers aren't quite that bleak. About 1500 petitions are "paid" petitions filed by attorneys; and most of the cases granted are from that number.[33] If that's accurate, we are talking nearly 5 percent.[34]

Let's look at why such a tiny percentage of cases are reviewed. According to United States Supreme Court Rule 10, the Court may grant a petition for certiorari only "for compelling reason," such as:

> (a) a United States court of appeals has *entered a decision in conflict with the decision of another United States court of appeals on the same important matter; has decided an important federal question in a way that*

---

[32] "That's some catch, that Catch-22," Yossarian observed. "It's the best there is," Doc Daneeka agreed. *See* Joseph Heller, *Catch-22* (1961).

[33] Michael Migiel-Schwartz, *Are Paid Petitions for Certiorari in Decline—Again?*, SCOTUS Blog, (July 13, 2023), https://www.scotusblog.com/2023/07/are-paid-petitions-for-certiorari-in-decline-again/.

[34] In addition, there are some instances when a state's highest court reviews an appeal without a request.

> *conflicts with a decision by a state court of last resort; or has so far departed from the accepted and usual course of judicial proceedings*, or sanctioned such a departure by a lower court, as to call for an exercise of this Court's supervisory power;
>
> (b) a state court of last resort has decided an important federal question in a way that conflicts with the decision of another state court of last resort or of a United States court of appeals;
>
> (c) a state court or a United States court of appeals has decided an important question of federal law that has not been, but should be, settled by this Court, or has decided an important federal question in a way that conflicts with relevant decisions of this Court.[35]

(Emphasis added.)

If you skipped that long quote, and I don't blame you if you did, here's the shorter version. The Supreme Court is interested in law development. Law development is what supreme courts do. To make this even clearer, the Court drops this nugget at the end of Rule 10:

> A petition for a writ of certiorari is rarely granted when the asserted error consists of erroneous factual findings or the misapplication of a properly stated rule of law.

That's another way of saying the Court won't grant an appeal for the sake of correcting an error. Error correction is what appellate courts do.

So, what's the lesson in seeking an appeal by permission?

---

[35] U.S. Sup. Ct. R. 10.

First, in the Supreme Court's mind, the trial court proceedings have concluded, and any errors were corrected on direct appeal.

Second, as we talked about earlier, make sure your request for review with the U.S. Supreme Court or a state's highest court has law development implications. Point out that the case involves a circuit split, a question of first impression, an issue of constitutional magnitude, or an issue of great public importance. (Ideally, more than one of those things.)

Finally, show that courts have struggled with how to resolve the issue and that a need for clarity and uniformity exists.

Here are a few recent examples. Notice how each one suggests a need for law development. In other words, the resolution of these cases will affect many more cases to follow.

- Whether the court of appeals erred in applying the guilt-based approach, rather than the error-based approach, to assess the harmlessness of the confrontation clause error; and whether, under *Apprendi v. New Jersey*, the facts underlying a restitution award must be proved to, and found by, a jury beyond a reasonable doubt.
- Whether the *Feres* doctrine conflicts with the plain language of the Federal Tort Claims Act and should thus be clarified, limited, or overruled.
- Whether the Supreme Court of California's narrow test for an "acquittal," limited only to circumstances where the record clearly shows that the judge correctly applied the substantial-evidence standard, conflicts with this court's precedent under the Fifth Amendment's double jeopardy clause.

Even if you have a solid law development issue, preparing and filing a petition for writ of certiorari with the U.S. Supreme Court is a complex undertaking that might merit its own *Short and Happy Guide*.[36] The good news is that the key components of any petition—the statement of facts, the issue presented, and the argument—are much like the components in any appellate brief. Therefore, every aspect of brief writing covered in this guide will help when seeking an appeal by permission from any court and after one is granted. (At no extra charge.)

> ***And One More Thing***
>
> Knowing that appellate advocacy is intertwined with appellate *process* is essential to identify issues, preserve issues, execute appeals, and avoid the many traps and pitfalls. When it's time to rule, the appellate court will have no choice but to address the merits of your arguments. That's how you give yourself a chance.

---

[36] If you don't believe me, here's an excerpt from Supreme Court Rule 33:

1. Booklet Format: (a) Except for a document expressly permitted by these Rules to be submitted on 81/2- by 11-inch paper, see, e. g., Rules 21, 22, and 39, every document fled with the Court shall be prepared in a 61/8- by 91/4-inch booklet format using a standard typesetting process (e. g., hot metal, photocomposition, or computer typesetting) to produce text printed in typographic (as opposed to typewriter) characters. The process used must produce a clear, black image on white paper. The text must be reproduced with a clarity that equals or exceeds the output of a laser printer.

U.S. Sup. R. 33.

PART TWO

First Impressions

CHAPTER III

Appellate Brief Components

An appellate brief must contain a table of authorities, a table of contents, a jurisdictional statement, a statement of the issues, a statement of the case, a statement of the facts, a summary of the argument, the argument, the standards of review, and a conclusion.[1] Be sure to include every component in the required

[1] Every legal writer employs at least one long footnote that readers probably won't read, so here's mine. The Federal Rules of Appellate Procedure require the appellant's brief to contain the following (in order):

> "(1) a disclosure statement if required by Rule 26.1; (2) a table of contents, with page references; (3) a table of authorities—cases (alphabetically arranged), statutes, and other authorities—with references to the pages of the brief where they are cited; (4) a jurisdictional statement, including: (A) the basis for the district court's or agency's subject-matter jurisdiction, with citations to applicable statutory provisions and stating relevant facts establishing jurisdiction; (B) the basis for the court of appeals' jurisdiction, with citations to applicable statutory provisions and stating relevant facts establishing jurisdiction; (C) the filing dates establishing the timeliness of the appeal or petition for review; and (D) an assertion that the appeal is from a final order or judgment that disposes of all parties' claims, or information establishing the court of appeals' jurisdiction on some other basis; (5) a statement of the issues presented for review; (6) a concise statement of the case setting out the facts relevant to the issues submitted for review, describing the relevant procedural history, and identifying the rulings presented for review, with appropriate references to the record (see Rule 28(e)); (7) a summary of the argument, which must contain a succinct, clear, and accurate statement of the arguments made in the body of the brief, and which must not merely repeat the argument headings; (8) the

order. We will save some of these components for later in the guide, but it's important to note that even the technical requirements make a first impression. Let's look at a few.

A. Cover Page

A court will *see* your brief before it *reads* your brief. Attention to detail will make an immediate statement about your professionalism and credibility. The cover of an appellate brief, for example, will include the names of the parties, the names of the lawyers, the docket numbers, the court, and other information. Make sure the docket numbers are accurate. Make sure the name of the court is correct. And please spell names correctly. Readers will notice errors.

Take it from a guy named B-a-r-c-k-h-o-f-f.

B. Jurisdictional Statement

The jurisdictional statement shows the basis for the district court and court of appeals' jurisdiction. For example, a district court may have federal diversity jurisdiction under 28 U.S.C. § 1332, and the court of appeals may have appellate jurisdiction under 28 U.S.C. § 1291. Relevant dates showing the timeliness of the appeal, e.g., the final judgment and the notice of appeal, might also be included. In short, show that your case is properly before the court.

---

argument, which must contain: (A) appellant's contentions and the reasons for them, with citations to the authorities and parts of the record on which the appellant relies; and (B) for each issue, a concise statement of the applicable standard of review (which may appear in the discussion of the issue or under a separate heading placed before the discussion of the issues); (9) a short conclusion stating the precise relief sought; and (10) the certificate of compliance, if required by Rule 32(g)(1)."

Fed. R. App. P. 28.

C. Table of Authorities and Citations

The table of authorities cites the primary and secondary authorities and shows the reader where the authority can be found in the brief. Because the table of authorities requires that each source be cited, this is a reminder to dust off your *Bluebook*. Don't worry, I wouldn't dare try to cover the particulars of citation principles in a *Short and Happy* guide even if I wanted to. (But we will look at a few things later on in this guide.) Suffice to say that lawyers and judges will see inconsistencies and proofreading errors when reading the entire brief. Worse, they will find cites that don't exist and references to pages that don't support the point being made. That's not good. Imagine having the court point out your errors like this:

> The appellant relies on *Crosby v. Malkin*, 500 F.5th 700, 702 (14th Cir. 2023), but that case cannot be found in that reporter. In fact, that case cannot be found in *any* reporter as it simply doesn't exist. This appears to be an instance where artificial intelligence does not substitute for actual intelligence and attention to detail. What's more, all the cases that *do* exist support the trial court's ruling, etc.

Okay, that was a little dramatic because we needed to spice up a chapter on technical components and citations. But take the time to cite authority correctly in the table of authorities, and you will likely do so throughout the brief. That adds professionalism and credibility to your work.

D. Table of Contents

The table of contents must indicate where each component of the brief may be found. It's also the first chance to show the reader the key portions of your argument. Remember, the technical parts of the brief make a first impression. Therefore, let's say that the table of contents simply tells the reader that "The Argument" begins on page ten of the brief. That's all most readers would expect.

But compare that to a table of contents that tells the reader that "The Argument" begins on page ten of the brief and contains the following headings and subheadings:

I. Assigning the Plaintiff to Administrative Segregation Following His Conviction for Capital Murder Did Not Violate the Fourteenth Amendment.

   A. Plaintiff did not establish a state created liberty interest because his assignment to administrative segregation did not impose an atypical and significant hardship compared to ordinary solitary confinement.

   B. Even if Plaintiff established a liberty interest, his interest in avoiding administrative segregation is minimal and substantially outweighed by the Government's interest in keeping death-sentenced inmates separate from the prison population.

II. Assigning the Plaintiff to Administrative Segregation Following His Conviction for Capital Murder Does Not Violate the Eighth Amendment.

   A. Conditions of plaintiff's confinement do not pose a substantial risk of significant harm because he has all of life's necessities, receives medical attention, and does not suffer from the wanton infliction of pain.

B. Even if a substantial risk of significant harm existed, there was no evidence prison officials were deliberately indifferent to the harm.

Wow. Without knowing *anything* about the facts or the law in advance, readers who glance at this page learn the nature of the action and the trial court's ruling. They see that the case involves capital murder and solitary confinement. They see that the two main issues involve the 14th and 8th amendments. They see the logic between subheadings A and B: "We win on A, and even if we don't win on A, we win on B." (Otherwise known as "heads we win; tails they lose.") That's a lot of information for someone who just happens to scroll through the table of contents.

Still with me? Here's another example.

I. The School District did not violate B.P.'s First Amendment right to free speech when he was suspended from school and dismissed from the football team based on his social media posts that disparaged the LGBTQ population.

A. Although B.P. used his own cellular phone in posting the remarks on a private social media site, they were substantially connected to the school because they were visible to his network of friends, shared with many more students, and targeted students who attend B.P.'s high school.

B. In addition to the substantial connection with school, B.P.'s posts resulted in a substantial disruption to school activities.

II. Even if B.P.'s posts were entitled to First Amendment protections, School District officials are shielded from civil liability under qualified immunity protections.

Once again, notice how much the reader learns from a single page in the table of contents. This is the School District's brief in a case involving the first amendment, a high school student, the use of social media, and the LGBTQ community. Issue I states that the School District did not violate the student's first amendment right; and even if it did, Issue II asserts school officials are entitled to immunity. Again, not a bad start!

E. Procedural History

The preliminary components of the brief should also tell the reader the procedural history. In federal appeals, the Statement of the Case includes the procedural history *and* the underlying narrative as well. In other jurisdictions, the Statement of the Case contains the procedural history, and a separate Statement of the Facts contains the underlying narrative.

Either way, there are things to remember when it comes to telling readers the procedural information. Be sure to include the following:

- The parties to the proceeding.
- The nature of the case.
- An overview of the pleadings.
- The dates of the underlying incident.
- An overview of the relevant motions and pretrial hearings.
- Trial court rulings.
- Judgments and verdicts.
- Post-trial motions.

- Entry of final judgment.
- Notice of appeal.
- The parties to the appeal.

With that information in mind, you can construct a concise procedural history that starts at the very beginning and ends with why the case is properly before the appellate court. In all but the most complex of appeals, a procedural overview should be relatively concise. Here are a few tips:

- Keep the procedural history relevant; you do not need to include the disposition of motions and objections that are not raised on appeal.
- Use specific dates sparingly. Reading an entire paragraph of sentences beginning with dates gets tiresome:

  > On April 1, 2023, the plaintiff filed a complaint for negligence. On May 1, 2023, the defendant filed an answer. On June 1, 2023, the plaintiff amended the complaint. On July 1, 2023, the defendant moved for summary judgment. A hearing was held on September 17, 2023. On October 15, 2023, a second hearing was held. On November 17, 2023, the trial court denied the motion for summary judgment. Etc.

  See? Unless the dates are relevant in some way—a timeliness issue, a statute of limitations, etc.—they can often be omitted.
- Focus on the parties involved in the appeal. Other parties or claims who have fallen out of the lawsuit at some point can be relegated to a footnote.

And One More Thing

The preliminary components of the brief are not only about complying with court rules, but also about making a first impression. Pay attention to the details. Will the reader skip the technical sections to get to the body of the brief? Yeah, most likely. But you should still do your best work, just in case.

CHAPTER IV

Statement of Facts

Everyone enjoys a good story. That's why we read books, watch movies, and spend too much money on streaming services. A brief must tell a compelling story with the facts that are found in the record on appeal. Let's repeat that last part: the facts found in the record on appeal.

A. Reviewing the Record on Appeal

We talked about the record earlier. The shorter version of that discussion is this: "If it's not in the record on appeal, it didn't happen." Underscoring the importance of the record is the requirement that every fact *asserted* in your brief must be accompanied by a citation to the record. Unless a court has a specific format, something like this will do:

(R. Vol. I at 125-132.)

(Trial Tr. Vol. 2 at 157-59.)

I can't tell you how many briefs I've read[1]—briefs filed by lawyers—that exceeded the scope of the record by referencing a letter, an

[1] I don't mean it's a big secret or anything. Let's say more than 10, fewer than 100.

affidavit, a statement, or some other document that was not introduced during the trial proceedings. Sometimes they even attached the document to the brief. But I can tell you that the extra material was of no use to anyone.

Reviewing the record to assemble a statement of the facts requires a close and careful reading of the pleadings, motions, and transcripts. If you get the impression that carefully reviewing the record may take a while, you're correct. Take notes as you read and have an idea of what to look for. What are you looking for?

- The parties and cast of characters. Who's who?
- The factual events. Who did what to who? Or whom.
- The legal themes and theories that were presented in the lower court. Why did everyone act the way they did?
- A summary of each witness's testimony, including key passages that may need to be quoted. Who saw what? Who said what?
- The testimony favorable to your client. Hopefully there's something good to say.
- The testimony unfavorable to your client. There will likely be something bad, especially for the appellant.
- The exhibits, documents, or records.

Once you have a handle on the content, the fun begins.

B. Storytelling

Trial lawyers tell stories through opening statements, evidence, and closing arguments. Appellate lawyers convey those stories in the statement of facts. A well-told story has a beginning, middle, and end. It identifies characters and creates a narrative. It emphasizes some facts and deemphasizes others. And it has a point of view. After all, someone has to tell the story, right?

Let's look at a short example of storytelling from an appellate brief. My comments are in italics.

> The Defendant was placed on trial for capital murder in Fayette County, Tennessee, a small rural county where he had lived with his wife of ten years and their two children. (R. Vol. I, 2-3.) A team of three lawyers prosecuted the case. One prosecutor was, of course, an Assistant District Attorney. But the other two were private practitioners who had been retained by the family of the deceased. (R. Vol. I at 4-7; Vol. II at 74.)

You probably guessed this is the Defendant's brief, right? The Defendant did not commit a murder; he was "placed on trial." He was a family man from a small county. He has two children. Let's see what happens.

> The two private practitioners were law partners who had been asked by the family of the deceased to help the State seek the death penalty. One private lawyer was the long-time chairman of the Republican party in what was a predominantly Republican County. His law partner was a member of the Executive Committee of the Democratic party for the State of Tennessee. Both men were popular and well-regarded in the community. Like all private practitioners, they owed professional obligations to their client. (R. Vol. II at 74-80.)

Did you know private attorneys can represent the victim's family in a criminal prosecution? I didn't. Does that make you want to keep reading?

> Acting pursuant to a so-called "Hired Gun" statute, which permits privately retained lawyers to help prosecute criminal cases, both men entered appearances as co-counsel with the District Attorney. (R. Vol. I at 4-7.) At the request of the deceased's family, the "private" prosecutors met with the District Attorney and urged the State to seek the death penalty. (R. Vol. I at 8.)
>
> They were successful.
>
> Just three weeks before the trial was to begin, the State filed a notice seeking the death penalty. The State cited a single aggravating circumstance in support of the death penalty, alleging that the single shot which was fired "knowingly created a great risk of death to two or more persons, other than the victim." Tenn. Code Ann. § 39-2-203(i)(3). (R. Vol. I at 4-7.)

The private attorneys convinced the prosecutor to seek the death penalty. What else did they do? Glad you asked.

> The two private attorneys took an active and vigorous role in the prosecution. Both participated in voir dire. (R. Vol. II at 100.) Both told the prospective jury that they represented the family of the deceased. (R. Vol. III at 168.) Both introduced the mother of the deceased to prospective jurors. (R. Vol. III at 168, 181.) Both called witnesses on behalf of the prosecution, and both participated in the cross-examination of defense witnesses. (R. Vol. IV at 292.) One private attorney made the state's opening statement while the second participated in the state's closing argument. (R. Vol. IV at 200-12; R. Vol. V. at 343.)

Hey, did you happen to notice that the Defendant was in the first sentence of the first paragraph and then disappeared? His narrative—his point of view—is about the trial procedure, the unique "hired gun" law, and the active role played by private lawyers retained by the victim's family.

> The case they prosecuted was tragically simple.

Two quick points. First, notice how this simple transition controls the narrative. We don't learn about the actual offense until we know the context. Second, the case is described as "tragically simple." That foreshadows what comes next.

> On Halloween night, the Defendant's wife and her sister-in-law took their children trick-or-treating by car through an affluent neighborhood. As they were leaving the neighborhood, they were pursued by the driver of a vehicle with a dark tinted windshield. Unable to see the driver or any other occupants, the Defendant's wife sought to flee the subdivision. (R. Vol. IV at 190-98.)

I don't know about you, but I feel like something bad is going to happen.

> The driver of the other car immediately gave chase, speeding up and flashing his high beam lights. When the Defendant's wife tried to pull into a convenience store to seek help, the pursuing car pulled in front of her, blocking her path. She heard the children "crying in hysteria," and she told them to "cling to the floorboard of the car." (R Vol. IV at 190-98.) After fleeing down the curving road that led to the trailer she shared with her husband, she drove through their front yard blowing the horn. (R. Vol. IV at 205-210.)

Had the narrative been a simple chronology of events, the story would likely start here. But that wouldn't have told the story that this defendant wanted to convey.

> The Defendant and his brother-in-law raced to the front door, saw the darkened car, and gave chase. They were unsuccessful. After returning to their trailer, the Defendant and his brother-in-law decided to return to the neighborhood where the original difficulty had arisen. As they were about to leave, the Defendant's wife handed her husband a loaded shotgun and warned him to be careful. She "was not sure if the people behind the tinted windows were armed and dangerous." (R. Vol. IV at 212.)

A loaded shotgun? Uh-oh.

> The Defendant located the house where the chase had begun and found the darkened car parked in the driveway. Angry that his wife and children had been placed in peril, he demanded to know why the driver of the other car had tried to kill his family. After a heated and emotional exchange ensued, the Defendant "attempted to scare the driver" by firing a shot between his legs. (R. Vol. IV at 245-50.) The single shot was fired downward at a 45-degree angle and caught the driver in the left hip. The shot at that close range, tragically, proved fatal. The wounded man died in the hospital three days later. (R. Vol. IV at 267; Vol. V at 415-20).

And here we are. The defendant was angry, engaged in a heated exchange with the victim, and fired a shot that resulted in the victim's death.

Using this example, let's talk more about storytelling

C. Points to Emphasize

1. Theme and Theory

The theme is a broad characterization about the case. We just saw an example of one: the defendant was unfairly prosecuted by a team that included an assistant district attorney and two private lawyers who represented the victim's family. If the prosecution had been telling the story, you can bet the theme had something to do with revenge and the shooting death of an unarmed teenager.

Think about themes in other kinds of cases. You've probably seen a movie or read a book with the same ideas.

- A product was defective due to shortcuts and corporate greed.
- A plaintiff's injuries were the result of their own negligence.
- The prosecution rushed to judgment despite a sloppy, incomplete investigation.
- A killing was motivated by jealousy or greed.
- A killing was in self-defense.
- An employer fired an employee for blowing the whistle on unlawful activity.
- A corporate defendant valued profits over safety.
- A defendant's conduct was the result of her blind ambition.
- A spouse demanded total control over the relationship.

The theme at trial is important because the appellate brief might pick up on those same ideas. At the very least, the reader should be able to identify who wrote the brief in the first paragraph or two. In the private prosecutor case described above, for example, the first paragraph identified the Defendant in the same sentence as his wife and two children. That laid the entire groundwork for his defense: protection of his family.

Here are two examples. Decide who wrote these opening paragraphs and what themes are introduced:

Example 1

> The plaintiff, Dr. Wellington Bartolomucci, PhD, is an exercise physiologist who has dedicated his entire 22-year career to helping individuals discover and build peak performance. From humble beginnings as a graduate assistant, Dr. Bartolomucci acquired years of education and experience to become a leader in the field of exercise science. More than a decade ago, he created the world's leading workout app, Peaking to Pros ("PTP"). PTP develops individualized workouts and diets for PTP members with the use of a unique algorithm developed by Dr. Bartolomucci between July 2015 and September 2017. PTP has grown to over four million members and accounts for nearly 8 percent of the market in the United States. Not surprisingly, competitors in the market—like the defendant in this case—have often tried to use Dr. Bartolomucci's methods and glom onto PTP's hard-earned success. (R. Vol, II at 325-28.)

Example 2

> Workout Pros and PTP are two exercise apps among an industry of dozens of sites that generate or provide physical workout or diet recommendations to app users. Like all such apps, PTP develops its programs based on a databank consisting of factors such as fitness goals, height and weight, BMI, and related information. Despite the extensive market, dozens of competitors, and numerous

> commonalities, PTP singled out Workout Pros and brought this claim of infringement. (R. Vol. II. at 312-18.)

Did you guess example 1 was PTP's brief? Notice the theme: others have tried to copy PTP's method and "glom on" to their "hard-earned success." In contrast, example 2 provides a sneak preview of the defense: all apps are the same.

Example 3

This example takes a slightly different approach:

> On December 27, 2020, Nancy James pulled up to the ATM connected to Kerry Federal Credit Union. (R. Vol. I at 2, 14.) *She inserted her bank card and entered her PIN.* (R. Vol. I at 2, 14-17.) *Before she entered an amount to withdraw, her passenger door opened. The Defendant got in the car with a gun.* He "demanded that [James] withdraw seven hundred fifty dollars ($750) from the ATM. *Fearfully, James did as she was told. The Defendant grabbed the money and fled.* Federal agents reviewed the bank's security footage, determined that the Defendant matched the description of a person suspected in several other ATM robberies, and launched a full-scale investigation. (R. Vol. II at 23-37.)

Given the Defendant's conduct, this is either the prosecution's brief or an unusual approach by defense counsel.

In short, the opening paragraph of a brief is like the opening paragraph in any book. It's an opportunity to introduce your client and other key characters. It's an opportunity to build upon the theme employed at trial. Most importantly, it's an opportunity to capture the reader's attention.

Remember that a reader will either keep reading your brief or put it down. There is no third option.

2. Short Sentences, Active Voice

Because the entire narrative should be easy to read, our second technique in creating a narrative focuses on short sentences. I mean, what's easier to read than a short sentence?

Nothing.

See what I did there? Short sentences are simple and clear. Many years ago, my daughter's middle school teacher apparently taught the class that a sentence must have fifteen to twenty words. That gave me an eye twitch for about a week.

In the private prosecutor example, most of the narrative was conveyed in short, clear sentences.

- A team of three lawyers prosecuted the case.
- Two of the lawyers were private practitioners who had been retained by the family of the deceased.
- Both men were popular and well-regarded in the community.
- They requested that the State seek the death penalty.
- They were successful.
- The case was tragically simple.

Not every sentence needs to be short, of course. The above paragraph about the ATM robberies contains sentences of various lengths that give the narrative a nice rhythm. Imagine what might happen otherwise:

> On December 27, 2020, Nancy James pulled up to the ATM. The ATM was connected to Kerry Federal Credit Union. (R. Vol. I at 2, 14.) *She inserted her bank card. She entered her PIN.* (R. Vol. I at 2, 14-17.) *Before she entered an amount to withdraw, her passenger door*

> *opened. The Defendant got in the car. He had a gun.* He "demanded that [James] withdraw seven hundred fifty dollars ($750) from the ATM. *Fearfully, James did as she was told. The Defendant grabbed the money. He fled.* Federal agents reviewed the bank's security footage. They determined that the Defendant matched the description of a person. That person was suspected in several other ATM robberies. They launched a full-scale investigation. (R. Vol. II at 23-37.)

To be fair, you might notice that "one fact per sentence" is an effective technique when examining a witness at trial. But it doesn't always make for great reading.

3. Add Details

Our third technique is the use of detail. As capital murder trials go, the facts in the private prosecutor example are sparse. But when the details were added, they had purpose and placed the reader at the scene.

- The Defendant's wife "managed to flee down the curving road that led to the trailer she shared with her husband."
- She "drove through their front yard blowing the horn."
- "The Defendant and his brother-in-law raced to the front door, saw the darkened car, and gave chase."
- The Defendant's wife handed him "a loaded shotgun" and "warned him to be careful."
- Dark tinted windows.
- Single shot.

Imagine the following murder case:

The victim was shot. The victim died. The Defendant confessed. The Defendant was convicted.

Now add the details:

> The Defendant shot the victim several times with a .45 caliber handgun. Two shots—fired from close range—pierced the victim's heart. Two other shots penetrated his lungs. The victim slowly bled to death while the Defendant fled the scene. When apprehended three weeks later, the Defendant admitted he killed the victim because the victim had an affair with the Defendant's estranged wife. The jury convicted him after only thirty minutes of deliberation.

Now *that's* a story. The sentences are still short, but they are punctuated by key details. You can tell immediately that this is the prosecution's brief.

Using that same case, let's say the Defendant is sentenced to solitary confinement. Here are the details:

> The Defendant remains in solitary confinement for twenty-three and one-half hours of each day. He is isolated in a cell "roughly the size of a standard parking space." There is no window. The bed has a thin mattress and a threadbare blanket. There is a "stainless-steel toilet and sink." The cell walls are solid white, and the floor is made of "pure concrete." There is no carpet.

A mix of short sentences and details allows the reader to conjure a stark mental image.

These techniques are not reserved for criminal cases. Short sentences, active voice, and vivid details are easily employed in other cases. Imagine a plaintiff who pursues a claim for invasion of privacy after being unknowingly recorded by the Defendant. You could simply conclude that he was harmed by the Defendant's actions. Or, you could add details.

> The video had disastrous effects on Mr. Miller's reputation, financial well-being, and personal life. Mr. Miller was exiled from his church where he had served as Deacon, and he was asked to relinquish his role in the local homeowners' association. His friends and coworkers ridiculed him or stopped talking to him altogether. His employer is withholding his annual bonus and considering his termination. Mr. Miller faces mental anguish for which he has sought treatment.

Now *that* has a point of view.

Along these same lines, imagine how you might employ a point of view when writing a narrative in the following scenarios:

- A plaintiff's injury and daily life after a catastrophic event.
- A client's life-long efforts developing a business.
- A series of acts and omissions that led to corporate malfeasance.
- The impacts of an environmental disaster.
- The detailed process leading to the formulation of a trademark or trade secret.
- The education and experience of a physician who has been sued for malpractice.
- An incident of medical malpractice with debilitating effects.
- Sexual harassment incidents that lead to an employee's firing.

And so on. Remember, if the evidence was introduced at trial and is in the record on appeal, it's fair game for the brief.

4. Word Choice

Short sentences and details tell the story. Word choice makes the story leap from the page. Look at this example again:

> The Defendant shot the victim several times with a .45 caliber handgun. Two shots—fired from close range—pierced the victim's heart. Two other shots penetrated his lungs. The victim slowly bled to death while the Defendant fled the scene. When apprehended three weeks later, the Defendant admitted he killed the victim.

These words jump from the page: "victim" "shot," "handgun" "fired," "pierced," "heart," "penetrated," "lungs," "bled," "death," "fled," and "killed."

Finding the right word, like most other brief-writing tasks, is a matter of trial, error, creativity, and synonyms:

- The defendant ~~defrauded, fooled~~, *tricked* its customers.
- The plaintiff ~~raises~~, ~~revisits~~, ~~regurgitates~~, *rehashes* old claims.
- The plaintiff ~~assumed the risk~~, ~~engaged in voluntary conduct~~, *brought this on himself.*
- The defendant ~~hit~~, ~~struck~~, *slammed* Mr. Johnson's car.
- Husband *lied* about his ~~*adultery, affairs, infidelity*~~, *cheating.*
- The defendant ~~ignored~~, ~~evaded,~~ *dodged* his fiduciary duties.

- The defendant ~~blames, accuses,~~ *castigates* everyone but himself.
- The evidence showed the revenue figures were ~~wrong~~, ~~fudged~~, *cooked*.

Finding the right words at the right time is gratifying because they pop like a Batman comic book: "Bam," "Pow," "Slam." But be careful. They should never be used to substitute for the facts.

5. Quotes and Descriptions

In many cases, nothing tells a story better than an eyewitness's description of the events, a victim's testimony about the serious injuries suffered, or the language used in a contract or document.

In the private prosecutor excerpt, recall that the Defendant's wife testified her children were "crying in hysteria," and she told them to "cling to the floorboard." Hard to improve upon that.

Here's another example that builds onto the solitary confinement passage we looked at earlier; notice that the key descriptions are quoted from the record.

> For over 35 years, the Defendant has spent twenty-three and one-half hours of each day isolated in a cell "roughly the size of a standard parking space." There is no window. The bed has a thin mattress and a "threadbare blanket." There is a "stainless-steel toilet and sink." The cell walls are white, and the floor is made of "pure concrete." There is no carpet. "Because of the Defendant's deteriorated mental health and efforts at self-harm", prison officials "took away his access to pencils and pens" and left him with "a few broken crayons." On weekends, he may receive a "pre-approved, no-contact visit with family or a religious leader." But in

> thirty-five years, the Defendant "has not received a single contact visit." (R. Vol. IV at 450-54.)

That must be the Defendant's brief, right? How do we know? The quoted material tells the story.

6. Headings, Complex Facts, and Multiple Sections

Many narratives have a logical separation between the procedural history and the underlying events. Others, like the private prosecutor example, contain two narratives—one about the trial and the other about the underlying offense. Still others may involve complex cases, multiple parties, multiple dates, or other details that are hard to ~~describe~~, ~~organize~~, juggle. Breaking a story into smaller parts with headings and subheadings allows the reader to absorb a little at a time. They may even thank you for that.

D. Points to Deemphasize

I know what you're thinking. What about facts in the record that aren't exactly helpful to the story you are telling? You can't change them. You shouldn't ignore them. But you can deal with them effectively.

1. Say Less

Maybe one of the hardest things for a lawyer to do: state what is needed and move on.

2. Say More

If you want the reader to skip something, put the material in a long sentence. It's possible—indeed, all too common—to construct a lengthy sentence designed to invite readers to gloss over potentially damaging material and focus their attention elsewhere, however momentarily; indeed, unless your name is William Faulkner, loading words into a sentence—even one that is grammatically correct—nearly always grinds the reader down by blending the words and phrases into the page, seen but not read, like the written equivalent of white noise.

See?

You would not want that to happen in a sentence containing material you want to emphasize. But if you put a long sentence in the middle of a long paragraph, well, see for yourself:

> Returning to the trailer, the Defendant and his brother-in-law decided to return to the suburb where the original difficulty had arisen. *As they were about to leave, the Defendant's wife handed her husband a loaded shotgun and warned him to be careful because she "was not sure if the people behind the tinted windows were armed and dangerous."* (R. Vol. IV at 212.) *The Defendant located the house where the chase had begun and found the darkened car parked in the driveway; angry that his wife and children had been placed in peril, he demanded to know why the driver of the other car had tried to kill his family and, after a heated and emotional exchange, "attempted to scare the driver" by firing a shot between his legs.* (R. Vol. IV at 245–50.) The single shot was fired downward at a 45-degree angle and caught the driver in the left hip. The shot at that close range, tragically, proved fatal. The wounded man died in the hospital three days later.

Somewhere in this paragraph a young man was shot and killed. Not only did this information appear later in the narrative, but some bad facts are also in the two long sentences in the middle of this paragraph.

Speaking of Faulkner. In *Requiem Practices*, Faulkner created a sentence—one sentence!—that contained over 12,000 words. *See* William Faulkner: *Narrative Practice and Prose Style* (1973). And no, I didn't read that sentence, and I sure didn't count the words. I suppose if ALL the facts in your case are bad for your client (hello, criminal defense lawyers) you could write the entire statement of facts in one sentence. But don't use 12,000 words. You only get 13,000 words for the entire brief. *See* Fed. R. App. P. 32(a)(7)(B)(i).

I'm rambling. Let's just move on.

3. Passive Voice

Passive voice can make facts look like they happened on their own. In the private prosecutor case, notice that the defendant does not appear in the most damaging part of the entire narrative:

> The single shot was fired downward at a 45-degree angle and caught the driver in the left hip. The shot at that close range, tragically, proved fatal. The wounded man died in the hospital three days later.

The Defendant has gone missing, and the shot apparently fired itself.

Here are a few more examples from other cases in which bad things seemingly happened on their own.

- Alcohol was consumed.
- Mistakes were made.
- There was infidelity in the marriage.
- A complaint for divorce was filed.

Those four sentences could be the story told by a bad spouse. "Hey, who really remembers what happened, let's just skip the details, and move on," they seem to be saying. Here are a few more.

- Shots were fired.
- Injuries were inflicted.
- The contaminated water found its way into the drinking supply.
- The tax forms were not sent.
- Payment was not made.
- Threats were made.
- Insults were exchanged.
- Accusations were levied.
- The samples were switched.
- Contractual obligations were not fulfilled.

Want more examples? Google "examples of passive voice." That's what I did.

- Google was used.
- Examples were found.

4. Context Matters

Often you can (and should) own the "bad" facts while putting them in a larger context

Recall this passage from our private prosecutor case:

> Returning to the trailer, the Defendant and his brother-in-law decided to return to the suburb where the original difficulty had arisen. As they were about to leave, the Defendant's wife handed her husband a loaded shotgun and warned him to be careful because she "was not sure if the people behind the tinted windows were armed and dangerous." (R Vol. IV at 212.)

Did the Defendant have a gun? Yes. But why? He believed that he and his family were in danger. And his wife was frightened.

> After a heated and emotional exchange ensued, the Defendant "attempted to scare the driver" by firing a shot between his legs. (R. Vol. IV at 245-50.) Although a single shot was fired downward at a 45-degree angle, it caught the driver in the left hip. The shot at that close range, tragically, proved fatal. The wounded man died in the hospital three days later.

Did the Defendant shoot the victim? Yes. But only "after a heated and emotional exchange." What does a "heated exchange" suggest? Both sides were involved and angry. Although a shot was fired, the Defendant wanted to scare the victim. How many shots were fired? Just one. Where was the victim struck? In the hip. Not the head or chest? No, just the hip. Was the entire event tragic? Of course.

Here are some additional examples. You can see how the "bad" facts are quickly surrounded by "good" ones.

- Although the defendant acknowledged that he drank two beers, he did so over the course of four hours. Not a single witness indicated he was intoxicated or even impaired.
- Although the trademarks were similar in shape and color, they were different in size, content, font, shading, material, and lettering.
- The plaintiff testified that he had come to a complete stop and looked both ways before turning right on red. Nearly every witness disputed his story. And two accident reconstruction experts concluded just the opposite.
- The victim testified that he fired his gun in self-defense because he thought the victim was armed.

He did not say anything of the sort when he made a statement to the police.

You get the idea. Think of this as damage control.

5. Long Quotes

Finally, long quotes will de-emphasize facts because everyone skips over them, particularly if they are singled spaced and double indented. And because they get skipped, I'm not putting any examples here.[2]

E. Examples

Here are some ideas to consider on your own.

Example 1

How would the private prosecutor narrative look from the State's point of view? What's the State's theme? Revenge? Shooting an unarmed victim from close range? What would you include in the first paragraph? How about these facts?

- Who shot the victim?
- What did he use to shoot the victim?
- How far away?
- How old was the victim?

What other things would you emphasize in the State's narrative?

- The Defendant and his family were safe at home.
- The Defendant chose to hunt down the victim.
- The Defendant took a shotgun.
- The shotgun was loaded.

---

[2] But if you *really* want an example, check out the footnote at the beginning of chapter three. You skipped that, right? Be honest. I know I would have.

- The Defendant drove around looking for the victim's car.
- The Defendant fired the shotgun at the victim from close range.
- The shot was fired into a car where the victim was sitting.
- The victim was unarmed.

In a nutshell, that's what the State's case is about. As for the private prosecutors, the State need only say they were allowed under state law and that they did not engage in misconduct.

Example 2

In this example, the Government's statement of the facts (with references to the record omitted for brevity) is compared with the Supreme Court's recitation of facts in *United States v. Tsarnaev*, 595 U.S. 302 (2022). As you may recall, the respondent in that case was convicted and sentenced to death for his role in the Boston Marathon bombing.[3] The Court of Appeals reversed[4] the sentence on an issue relating to pretrial media coverage and jury selection. The Government appealed.[5] Notice the similarities between the Government's brief and the Supreme Court's opinion. I've divided the excerpts into smaller parts. Notice the techniques we have discussed.

- **The respondent's actions leading to the bombing.**

Government:

On April 15, 2013, respondent and his brother Tamerlan—a fellow jihadist—walked to the crowded finish-line area of the Boston Marathon with backpacks

---

3 *Id.* at 311.

4 *Id.*

5 *Id.* at 312.

containing homemade pressure-cooker shrapnel bombs filled with BBs and nails. They separated, and each of them found a spot packed with spectators to place his bomb. Respondent selected the sidewalk near the crowded outdoor patio at the Forum restaurant, just behind several children watching the race. The brothers spoke on the phone, and about 20 seconds later, Tamerlan's bomb exploded. J.A. 164. The respondent then moved away from his own bomb, which exploded a few seconds later.

Court:

On April 15, 2013, the brothers went to the Boston Marathon finish line on Boylston Street. They each brought a backpack containing a *homemade pressure-cooker bomb packed with explosives inside a layer of nails, BBs, and other metal scraps.* Tamerlan left his backpack in a crowd of spectators and walked away. Dzhokhar stood with his backpack outside the Forum, a nearby restaurant where spectators watched the runners from the sidewalk and dining patio. For four minutes, Dzhokhar surveyed the crowd. *After speaking with Tamerlan by phone, Dzhokhar left his backpack among the spectators. Tamerlan then detonated his bomb. While the crowd at the Forum looked toward the explosion, Dzhokhar walked the other way. After a few seconds, he detonated his bomb.*

- **The damage inflicted.**

Government:

The bombs caused devastating injuries that left the street with "a ravaged, combat-zone look." "Blood and body parts were everywhere," littered among "BBs, nails, metal scraps, and glass fragments." "The smell of smoke and burnt flesh filled the air," and "screams of panic and pain echoed throughout the site." The first bomb "completely mutilated" the legs of race spectator Krystle Campbell, causing her to bleed to death on the sidewalk while her friend attempted to comfort her. Respondent's bomb "filleted" the leg of Boston University student Lingzi Lu "open down to the bone." People nearby worked frantically to save Lu's life and pleaded with her to "[s]tay strong," but she died within minutes. Respondent's bomb "also sent BBs and nails tearing through" the body of eight-year-old Martin Richard, "cutting his spinal cord, pancreas, liver, kidney, spleen, large intestine, and abdominal aorta, and nearly severing his left arm." The boy "bled to death on the sidewalk—with his mother leaning over him, trying to will him to live." The bombs also "consigned hundreds of others to a lifetime of unimaginable suffering." Among many other severe injuries, victims lost limbs, their sight, or their hearing. Respondent's bomb alone caused eight people—including Martin Richard's six-year-old sister—to lose their legs. The bomb also gashed the stomach of Lingzi Lu's friend so severely that she had "to hold her insides in."

Court:

Each detonation sent fire and shrapnel in all directions. The blast from Tamerlan's bomb shattered *Krystle Campbell's* left femur and mutilated her legs. Though bystanders tried to save her, she bled to death on the sidewalk. Dzhokhar's bomb ripped open the legs of *Boston University student Lingzi Lu. Rescuers tried to stem the bleeding by using a belt as a makeshift tourniquet. She too bled to death.*

Eight-year-old Martin Richard absorbed the full blast of Dzhokhar's bomb. BBs, nails, and other metal fragments shot through his abdomen, cutting through his aorta, spinal cord, spleen, liver, pancreas, left kidney, and large intestines. The blast propelled the shrapnel with such force that it exited his back. Other shrapnel nearly severed his left hand. The explosion also caused third-degree burns. Martin ultimately died from blood loss. *Dzhokhar's and Tamerlan's bombs maimed and wounded hundreds of other victims. Many people lost limbs, including Martin's 6-year-old sister, Jane.* Many more would have died if not for the swift action of citizens and first responders.

- **The respondent's actions after the bombing.**

Government:

Back at college the next day, respondent again accessed the electronic al Qaeda magazine with bomb-making instructions. That evening, he worked out at the gym with a friend and tweeted, "I'm a stress-free kind of guy." Three days later, the Federal Bureau of Investigation (FBI) released surveillance-camera images of the bombing suspects and asked the public to help find them. When a friend recognized respondent as one of the bombers and messaged him, he replied, "Better not text me my friend" and "Lol [laughing out loud]." That night, the respondent met up with Tamerlan again and they loaded pipe bombs, a handgun, and another shrapnel bomb into Tamerlan's car.

Court:

After fleeing the scene, the brothers returned to their normal lives. *Dzhokhar attended his college classes the next day. He went to the gym with friends. He posted online that he was "a stress-free kind of guy."* Several days later, on April 18, after the Federal Bureau of Investigation (FBI) released images of the suspected bombers, a friend saw the images and texted Dzhokhar. *Dzhokhar responded: "Better not text me my friend. Lol."* Recognizing that investigators were closing in on them, Dzhokhar met up with Tamerlan that evening. The brothers collected more homemade bombs and a handgun and loaded them into Tamerlan's car.

- **The respondent's manifesto and capture.**

Government:

Respondent abandoned the SUV about two blocks away, then fled a short distance on foot and hid in a covered boat behind a home. While inside the boat, respondent carved the words "Stop killing our innocent people, and we will stop." He also used a pencil to write out a manifesto to "shed some light on [his] actions." He stated that while "killing innocent people" is "forbidden in Islam" and he did not "like" it, "due to said [obscured] it is allowed." He accused "[t]he U.S. government [of] killing our innocent civilians" and stated that he could not "stand to see such evil go unpunished." He warned that "the [M]ujahideen" "ha[d]awoken," and that "you are fighting men who look into the barrel of your gun and see heaven." Ibid. He also wrote that he was "jealous" of Tamerlan's martyrdom and "ask[ed] Allah to make [him] a" martyr as well.

Court:

Dzhokhar abandoned the SUV a few blocks away. He found a covered boat in a nearby backyard. Taking shelter

> *inside, he carved the words "stop killing our innocent people, and we will stop" into the planking. He also wrote a manifesto in pencil on the bulkhead of the boat's cockpit justifying his actions and welcoming his expected martyrdom.* The next day, the boat's owner found him. Police eventually forced Dzhokhar out of the boat and arrested him.

Did you notice the techniques for emphasis? Make a list of short sentences, active voice, details, quotes, and vivid word choice. You'll find them all in there. Can you think of ways in which the respondent could have minimized those facts?

Did you also notice the parallels between the Government's brief and the Court's recitation of facts? They follow the same sequence, beginning with the respondent's commitment to jihad and his actions before the bombing. They name the victims and describe their horrific injuries. Both the Government and the Court note that the respondent called himself a "stress-free" guy. He texted a friend "not to text him, lol." Both contain the same details, right down to the pencil used to write the manifesto in the boat.

With only that information in mind, do you want to guess which side prevailed in the Supreme Court?[6]

[6] For more examples along these lines, *see* Maureen Johnson, *You Had Me at Hello: Examining the Impact of Powerful Introductory Emotional Hooks Set Forth in Appellate Briefs filed in Recent Hotly Contested U.S. Supreme Court Decisions*, 49 Ind. L. Rev. 397, 399 (2016) (Studying briefs that "began with an emotional 'hello' that would be hammered-home again and again throughout the brief and would make its way into the Supreme Court opinion").

And One More Thing

Will you win or lose based solely on the statement of facts? Probably not. But can you use them to make an impact? The Boston Bomber example suggests you can. Here's another way to look at it. You have one chance to write a brief on behalf of your client. That brief contains one statement of the facts. You have plenty of tools at your disposal.

Make the opportunity count.

CHAPTER V

What Are the Issues?

Like a compelling statement of facts, the statement of the issues offers an opportunity for the brief to make an impact. Look, it is *not* easy to make an impact on an audience that reads hundreds of appellate briefs for a living.[1] But it can be done. All you need to do is decide what issues *might* be raised, what issues *will* be raised, and how the issues will be *phrased*.

A. What Issues Might Be Raised?

The appellate court's role is to correct any errors made by the trial court. Therefore, your job is to show that errors were made and that the errors affected the outcome. Where do we start? You guessed it.

1. *The Record*

You must slowly and carefully review the record; remember if it's not in the record, the appellate court will conclude it didn't happen. Going through the record is easier if you were involved in

[1] "Look" is one of the three most annoying ways to start a sentence. The other two are "Listen" and "Don't kid yourself." I'll try not to make a habit of it. But listen, don't kid yourself.

the case from the beginning. But even if you come aboard for the appeal, no problem. There's nothing wrong with someone taking a fresh look.

2. The Pleadings

They will identify the claims, the defenses, the parties, and the allegations. If something or someone is not in there, they may as well not exist.

3. Pretrial Motions

Next, make a list of the pretrial motions that were filed. Take notes on where they are found in the record. See if a motion required the trial court to hear evidence or argument in a pretrial hearing. The court is required to rule on pretrial motions before the trial unless there's a good reason to defer ruling. And when factual issues are involved, the trial court should hold an evidentiary hearing and make findings on the record.[2]

4. Trial Transcript

Review the transcript and testimony. Remember our discussion about Federal Rule of Evidence 103? Look for objections that were made at trial and the trial court's rulings or written orders. Look for any offers of proof that were made. Match the trial transcript to any exhibits that were introduced.

5. Post-Trial Motions

Review the post-trial motions for timeliness and content. In a jurisdiction that requires issues to be preserved in a motion for a

---

[2] *See* Fed. R. Crim. P. 12(d) ("Ruling on a Motion. The court must decide every pretrial motion before trial unless it finds good cause to defer a ruling. The court must not defer ruling on a pretrial motion if the deferral will adversely affect a party's right to appeal. When factual issues are involved in deciding a motion, the court must state its essential findings on the record.").

new trial, you might even start your review of the record by reviewing that motion. Match the post-trial motions to the rulings made by the trial court.

6. *What's Not in the Record*

Now here's the fun part. As you review the record, try to identify any motions that *should* have been filed or any objections that *should* have been made. You or another lawyer at trial may have missed or overlooked them. That happens. Decisions are often made on the fly. It's possible to find issues that can be raised as plain error. Or perhaps the law has changed. Or maybe the law *should* be changed, or revised, or modified.

B. What Issues Will Be Raised?

With any luck—and more importantly, good work by the trial lawyer—you should generate a list of issues that were identified, raised, and preserved in the trial court. And you also may have a list of issues that were not identified, raised, or reserved in the trial court. You should have a list of where these things can be found in the record. And you should have a list of the trial court's rulings and where *those* can be found in the record.

So far, so good. But just because you *have* a list of issues does not mean you should *raise* them all. To decide which issues to present in the appellate brief, you must consider several more things.

1. *Update the Research*

Assess the strength of each possible issue by *updating the legal research* in support of your position as competently and diligently as possible. *The importance of legal research cannot be emphasized enough.* Motions and objections are often raised in good faith in the moment. That does not mean they've aged well. They may not have been researched exhaustingly in the first place. Or something may have changed since then. Take a new, honest look.

And don't forget, updating the research includes a close look at the authority cited by the opposing party or the lower court. On that note, remember that you cannot knowingly fail to disclose controlling authority that is directly adverse to your position. You may try to distinguish it or deal with it. But you have to disclose it. That's part of the professional duty of candor lawyers owe to the court.[3]

2. *Standard of Review*

Next, assess the strength of each issue under the applicable *standard of review*. When motions are filed and objections are made, the focus is getting the trial judge to agree. Now, the focus is on the appellate court's review of the trial court's ruling. And that's a new dynamic.

The good news is that every jurisdiction has well developed rules and case law to set out their standards of review. Here are a few examples to get you started.

a. For many of the trial court's procedural or evidentiary rulings, the standard of review on appeal is **abuse of discretion**. The appellate court extends great deference to the trial court. It's not enough that the appellate court may disagree with the trial court; it must conclude that the trial court abused its discretion. That generally requires the appellant to show the trial court applied the wrong standard, misconstrued a point of law, or failed to consider relevant and material facts.

[3] *See* MODEL RULES OF PRO. CONDUCT r. 3.1(b) (AM. BAR ASS'N 1983).

b. In contrast, if the trial court's ruling involves a question of law, the standard of review on appeal is ***de novo***. The appellate court does not defer to the trial judge's ruling. That can strengthen an argument if for no other reason than the appellate court has a blank slate.

c. If the issue involves a question of fact or a jury verdict, the standard of review on appeal is ***extremely deferential***. An appellate court will defer to the trial judge's factual findings unless they are clearly erroneous. And it will defer to a jury verdict whenever "any rational trier of fact could find the elements beyond a reasonable doubt." I won't say you're more likely to win the lottery than see a reversal of a jury's verdict. But you get the idea.

d. If the issue is a mixed question of fact and law, the appellate court will defer to the trial court's findings of fact but will not defer to the trial court's conclusions of law. You see that with suppression issues, for example.

Oh, and one more thing. The time spent looking up and considering the standard of review for each issue is well spent. As noted way back in chapter three, the parties are required to include the standard of review for every issue in their appellate briefs.[4] So, there's that.

3. Effect of the Error

Next, assess the strength of the issue with its effect on the result. Even if the trial court has erred under the applicable

---

[4] *See* Fed. R. App. P. 28(a)(8)(B).

standard of review, the appellant must show that the error merits relief.

a. Reversible Error

For an issue that was raised and preserved properly, the appellant must show that the trial court made an error and that the error more likely than not affected the outcome of the proceedings.[5] This requires an assessment of the error along with the strength of the evidence.

Let's say the trial court erred in refusing to allow impeachment of a witness. If that error occurred in a case that required the trier of fact to assess the credibility of two key witnesses, you have a strong argument that the error more likely than not affected the result. Similarly, the effect of a trial court's error may be magnified in a case involving mostly circumstantial evidence. Without that error, the trier of fact, more likely than not, may have reached a different result.

b. Constitutional Error

If a criminal defendant demonstrates that a constitutional error occurred, the government must show that the error was harmless beyond a reasonable doubt.[6] In other words, the burden is not only higher, it also shifts to the government. So, for example, if a defendant establishes that the trial court erred by allowing the government to use his involuntary confession at trial, the government will have to show that the error was harmless beyond a reasonable doubt. To do so, the government nearly always tries to argue that the evidence of guilt was strong even without the error. And honestly, the appellate court often agrees. How do we know

---

[5] *See* Fed. R. Crim. P. 52(a); Fed. R. Civ. P. 61.

[6] *Chapman v. California*, 385 U.S. 18 (1967).

that? Go back to the introduction and look at the affirmance numbers.

In rare cases, an error is not subject to harmless error analysis because it "affects the fundamental integrity" of the trial.[7] Examples include the total deprivation of the right to counsel, the failure to instruct the jury on reasonable doubt, the denial of an impartial jury, racial discrimination in the selection of the grand jury, and maybe a few others. But that's pretty rare.

c. Plain Error

If an issue was not preserved—not raised before or during trial, for instance—the appellant must show plain error. This means that an error was clear or obvious, that the error affected the appellant's substantial rights, and that the error had a serious effect on the fairness or integrity of the proceedings.[8]

As you may have gathered, any showing of reversible error is an uphill battle. A showing of plain error is even steeper. But if you recognize that an issue was not preserved, you can at least give yourself a chance by addressing plain error under the proper standards. Even if you don't get relief, you will likely gain credibility with the court. And, you know, that's nice.

4. *Ordering the Issues*

Think about the *order* in which to raise the issues. As always, there are plenty of considerations. Here are just a few.

a. Strongest Issue First

In a case with multiple issues, conventional wisdom says to present your strongest issue first. Surprise! Deciding which issue is the strongest is a function of everything we discussed above,

---

7 *Weaver v. Massachusetts*, 571 U.S. ___ (2017).

8 *See* Fed. R. Crim. P. 52.

particularly the legal research. If there's a case in which relief has been granted on a similar issue, that may well be your strongest issue. In other cases, an issue involving a question of law may be the strongest issue because the appellate court's review is *de novo*.

b. Context

Is there an issue that provides the backdrop for everything else that happened? In criminal cases, defendants often challenge the sufficiency of the evidence. Not because they will prevail on *that* issue; they rarely do. But that discussion may suggest that the evidence—though sufficient—was far from overwhelming. As the brief moves on to other issues, the appellant can argue that any alleged errors occurred in a case where the evidence against the defendant was hotly contested or marginal in some way. And if the court agrees an error was committed, the appellant has a head start on showing reversible error.

c. Chronological

The trial court erred from day one and the errors just kept coming, compounding their effect on the proceedings.

d. Logical

Think of this as "heads we win, tails they lose."

> Issue One: The complaint was barred by the statute of limitations.
>
> Issue Two: Even if not barred by the statute of limitations, the complaint failed to state a claim for relief.
>
> Issue Three: Even if the complaint stated a claim, the evidence did not reflect a genuine factual dispute necessary to avoid summary judgment for the defendant.

Issue Four: Even if summary judgment was not appropriate, the trial court erred with respect to evidentiary rules at trial.

And so on.

C. How Will the Issues Be Phrased

Now that you have identified and assessed the possible issues, think about how they should be worded. A few pages ago, I said that the statement of the issues "is an opportunity for the brief to make an impact." (That's right, I just quoted myself.) How do we capitalize on that opportunity? Here are some initial things to keep in mind.

First, a well-crafted statement of the issue combines a legal principle with legally relevant facts. You might even (politely) suggest the answer you want the court to reach.

Second, a well-crafted statement of the issue requires time and effort. I don't know anyone who can phrase the issue correctly in a rough draft. In fact, the precise content and the phrasing of your issues may not come into focus until after you have completed some legal research and written some of the argument.

Third, a well-crafted statement of the issue is written with the audience in mind. Judges may read the issues before they read any other part of the brief. And the judge's law clerk will definitely read the issues when summarizing the case for the court.

Therein lies the opportunity. If you draft a compelling statement of the issues and the other side does not, you may establish the terms of the debate.

"Ah-ha," I hear you saying. "But how?"

1. *Traditional Method for Stating the Issue*

Most of us learned the traditional method of phrasing a legal issue at the very beginning of law school. Start with the word "whether," identify a legal principle, add some legally relevant facts, and, above all else, hope you don't get called on in class. That same format is often used to create a traditional statement of the issue in an appellate brief, along with a few other guidelines. Here's a formula:

Whether + Law + Where + Legally Relevant Facts

Here's the thing. As you add legal principles and relevant facts you often lose clarity. That's fine. The precise phrasing often comes into focus only after much of the brief has been researched, analyzed, written, and refined. The point is to come back to the task and keep trying. In the meantime, here are some things to look out for.

a. Saying Too Little

One pitfall in drafting a statement of the issue is settling for a cryptic little placeholder that could fit any number of cases:

- Whether the trial court erred?

This is the issue in literally every case ever appealed in the history of recorded jurisprudence.

- Whether the trial court erred by denying the motion to suppress?

Better. By identifying a motion to suppress, the issue has been narrowed to about seven million possibilities under the 4th, 5th, and 6th amendments.

- Whether the search violated the Fourth Amendment?

We are now down to six million possibilities. But we don't know anything about the many facets of the Fourth Amendment or the facts of your case.

- Whether the warrantless search of the defendant's car violated the Fourth Amendment?

Much better. But we still don't know any facts about the case. Was the car searched during a traffic stop? Was the car stopped based on an anonymous tip? Was the driver detained while a drug dog was brought to the scene? And so on.

Many issue statements fail because they don't tell the reader anything useful. Well, that's not entirely true. They may tell the court that you haven't fully considered the legal principles and key facts of your case.

Some lawyers will compensate for the missing content by writing the issue in ALL CAPS:

WHETHER THE TRIAL COURT ERRED?

Please. Don't.

Do they serve as substantive legal muscle? No. Are they annoying to read? YES. Do they suggest a need for anger management? Possibly.

b. Saying Too Much

The opposite problem is trying to tell the reader everything. Rather than rethinking and revising the issue, a lawyer will throw everything into the mix and hope the court sorts it out. Here's an issue I once found in a brief written by a member of the bar (and I'm not kidding):

> Whether the Prosecution improperly severed two counts involving the exact same conduct (in this matter, one count of "Especially Aggravated Robbery" and one count

> of "Aggravated Kidnapping") in two separate indictments despite the fact that they should have been joined under mandatory joinder under Tennessee Rules of Criminal Procedure Rule 8(a), is the Prosecution obligated to dismiss the nonjoined charge ("Aggravated Kidnapping") prior to the Defendant's trial for "Especially Aggravated Robbery" to avoid tainting the Defendant's trial in that evidence of the second charge (for which the Defendant had not yet been tried for) with unfair prejudice, thus denying the Defendant's right to a fair and impartial trial under the U.S. and Tennessee Constitutions?

I don't know about you, but my brain broke around line four, and I blacked out before I got to the end. Maybe it turned out okay, but I doubt it. Think of this as the turning blue test: if you try to read an issue out loud in one breath and turn blue in the face for lack of air, it's too long.

All is not lost, though. This example was taken from a brief written by a practicing attorney, so you should feel pretty good about your chances to pass the bar exam.

c. Finding the Balance

Avoid extremes. Strive for something that is substantive, clear, and concise. I suggest using brackets to break the task into two distinct parts: put the legal principles in the first set of brackets and the legally relevant facts in a second set. That ensures you don't omit anything and forces you to be concise. If you have an empty bracket, you forgot something.

Here are some examples:

- Whether [a confession was voluntary under the 5th and 14th amendments] where [the defendant was questioned for four days, denied food and water, and beaten with barbed wire].

- Whether [the trial court erred in awarding a divorce and alimony to Wife] where [Husband was mentally abusive, emotionally cruel, and a serial adulterer].
- Whether [testimony was admissible as an excited utterance under Fed. R. Evid. 803] where [the declarant saw a man who was wearing a hockey mask and holding a chainsaw and immediately shouted "quick, let's hide in the cemetery!"].
- Whether [the employer violated Title VI and VII] where [they fired an employee who had reported senior management's culture of drug use and sexual harassment].

In each of these examples, it's the information in the second set of brackets that speaks to your specific case. Because appellate judges know a lot about the law, the facts are the part that makes an impact.

d. Take out Clutter

What's clutter? Anything that gets in the way and distracts the reader from the legal principle and relevant facts. If you can take out a word or phrase and the rest stands on its own, then leave it out. Procedural history and dates often stand out as clutter.

- "Whether the Court of Appeals erred by reversing the trial court, which had concluded blah, blah, blah. . . ."
- "Whether the Government violated the Defendant's rights as stated in the Fourth Amendment of the United States Constitution and as upheld by the United States Supreme Court ever since *Mapp v. Ohio*, blah blah blah. . . ."

- "Whether the mandatory requirements clearly and expressly set forth in section 1313 of the United States Code Annotated, were satisfied where blah, blah, blah. . . ."
- "Whether the trial court properly granted summary judgment under Rule 56 of the Federal Rules of Civil Procedure in favor of the Defendant, Lamar Corporation (hereinafter "Lamar"), where blah blah blah. . . ."
- Whether the plaintiff's complaint filed on April 1, 2020, was improperly dismissed upon the motion for summary judgment filed by the defendant on August 15, 2020, etc.

Simply put, the more you can take out stuff that doesn't matter, the more room you will have for stuff that does. Notice how this works in the following examples.

Example 1

Before:

Whether ~~Court of Appeals erred in affirming the trial court's ruling that~~ the defendant's right to counsel under the Sixth Amendment ~~to the United States Constitution and the United States Supreme Court's decision in the case of *Illinois v. Kirby*~~ was violated when he was arrested for conspiracy and ~~thereafter subsequently~~ questioned by an undercover FBI agent?

After:

Whether the defendant's Sixth Amendment right to counsel was violated when he was arrested for conspiracy and then questioned by an undercover FBI agent?

By taking out references to the Court of Appeals, the trial court, the United States Constitution, and the Supreme Court case, we went from six lines to three. And by creating that extra space, you could keep the reference to *Illinois v. Kirby* if you *really* want to.

Example 2

Before:

Whether ~~the Court of Appeals should have affirmed the decision of the lower court~~ that an expert witness's testimony violated the ~~Sixth Amendment~~ Confrontation Clause r~~ights of a criminal defendant~~ when he relied, ~~in part,~~ on a former colleague's notes and analysis from the same crime lab to reach an independent opinion but was subject to cross examination at trial?

After:

Whether an expert witness's testimony violated the Confrontation Clause when he relied on a former colleague's notes and analysis from the same crime lab to reach an independent opinion but was subject to cross examination at trial?

Again, taking out stuff that doesn't matter allows the reader to see the material that does.

Example 3

Before:

Whether the Sixth Circuit corrected reversed the trial court's ruling that the Government's compelling a defendant to reveal the numerical passcode to his locked cell phone is a violation of his right against self-incrimination under the Fifth Amendment to the United States Constitution

> After:
>
> Whether the Fifth Amendment right against self-incrimination prohibits the Government from compelling a defendant to reveal the numerical passcode to his locked cellphone?

Just a few revisions can make a lot of difference.

e. Suggest the Answer

Now let's add a wrinkle. Can you make a statement of the issue stronger by somehow suggesting the answer you want the court to reach? The answer is twofold: (1) sometimes; but (2) be careful. We do not want to turn the issues into arguments, so something like this would not work:

> Whether the evidence was sufficient to support first degree murder where the defendant acted with premeditation and intent when killing the victim.

But this might:

> Whether the evidence was sufficient to support first degree murder where the defendant threatened to kill the victim, purchased a handgun, waited in a closet, and shot the victim five times in the chest from close range.

See the difference? The first one states conclusions; the second one states facts about what the defendant actually *did*. What's more, if the defendant actually *did* those things, that sure seems like first-degree murder to me. Here's another example:

> Whether Tennessee's mandatory sentence of life imprisonment violates the Eighth Amendment when imposed on a juvenile offender for first-degree murder?

As "before" examples go, that's not too bad. The issue contains the legal principle—Eighth Amendment—and a few facts—mandatory life sentence imposed on a juvenile for first degree murder. The issue is concise and easy to read. But let's again add a wrinkle by subtly suggesting the answer:

> Whether Tennessee's mandatory sentence of life imprisonment for a juvenile convicted of first-degree murder—which is contrary to every other State in the country—violates the Eighth Amendment?

Now the reader knows that Tennessee's sentence, for whatever reason, is an outlier. That draws attention. That makes an impact.

f. Putting It All Together

Now you try. Read the passage and fill in the brackets.

The defendant, age 15, is questioned for four hours without a break. Officers tell him he will not be charged if he "tells the truth." Defendant admits that he broke into the home of Wally Squally. The 14th amendment to the United States Constitution requires that confessions be voluntary. The trial court looked at the totality of the circumstances and ruled that the confession was voluntary.

Issue: Whether [legal principles] where [facts].

For a will to be valid under Ames Code Annotated § 38-17-1034, two witnesses must attest that they saw the testator sign the will in their presence. In this case, one witness, Jack Daniels, watched the testator sign the will. A second witness, James Beam, was taking a call in an adjoining office. Beam did not see the testator sign the will, but he saw the signature on the page moments later. No one else had entered or left the room. The trial court ruled that the will was invalid because the will was not signed in the presence of the second witness.

Issue: Whether [legal principles] where [facts].

2. *Alternative Method for Stating the Issue*

A popular alternative breaks the task into more manageable parts.

First, draft a sentence that captures the core legal principle about your issue. You don't have to cite authority, but you must be absolutely accurate. If you struggle to articulate a concise rule in one sentence, that's fine. You may just need more research and interpretation. Like I said, drafting the issues takes time.

Second, draft a sentence or two about the key facts. What one or two things do you need the reader to know about your case?

Third, pose the question.

Let's use this technique with some of the passages we reviewed earlier.

Before:

> Whether Court of Appeals erred in affirming the trial court's ruling that the defendant's right to counsel under the Sixth Amendment to the United States Constitution and the United States Supreme Court's decision in the case of *Illinois v. Kirby* was violated when he was arrested for conspiracy and thereafter subsequently questioned by an undercover FBI agent?

After:

> The Sixth Amendment right to counsel attaches after a defendant has been formally charged. The Defendant was arrested for conspiracy, booked, and released on bail. Two weeks later, he was questioned for over two hours by an undercover FBI agent without the presence of counsel.

> Did the trial court err in denying the Defendant's motion to suppress his statement?

By removing some clutter and using the alternative approach, we can sneak in a few more facts that suggest the answer.

> Before:
>
> Whether Tennessee's mandatory sentence of life imprisonment violates the Eighth Amendment when imposed on a juvenile offender for first-degree murder?
>
> After:
>
> A mandatory sentence imposed on a juvenile offender violates the Eighth Amendment where it is disproportionate, serves no valid objective, and fails to consider the mitigating factor of youth. Unlike every other jurisdiction in the US, Tennessee automatically sentences juveniles convicted of first-degree murder—like the Defendant—with no consideration of age or other mitigating factors. Is the sentence cruel and unusual under the Eighth Amendment?

I know what you're thinking. "Hey Barckhoff, isn't that alternative longer than the traditional method?" Well, yes. But the length stems from additional material that suggests the answer.

> Before:
>
> Whether the Fifth Amendment right against self-incrimination prohibits the Government from compelling a defendant to reveal the passcode to his cellphone?
>
> After:
>
> The Fifth Amendment prohibits the Government from compelling a person to provide incriminating testimonial statements. The Defendant's cellphone was seized in connection with the Government's investigation into a

> burglary ring. Although the Government obtained a search warrant for the cellphone, the Defendant refused to provide the passcode for agents to review the contents of the phone. Did the trial court err by denying the Government's motion to compel?

Once again, the "after" version contains more information without sacrificing clarity and readability.

As you can see from these examples, the alternative structure allows you to break things into smaller parts. Rather than a weird sentence that begins with the word whether, the reader can handle one clear sentence at a time. Ideally, when the reader gets to the question, they will have the answer.

Here are the earlier examples to try on your own.

> The defendant is questioned for four hours without a break. Officers tell him he will not be charged if he "tells the truth." Defendant admits that he broke into the victim's home. The 14th amendment requires that confessions be voluntary. The trial court ruled that the confession was voluntary.
>
> Legal Principle: ____________________
>
> Key Facts: ____________________
>
> Question: ____________________
>
> For a will to be valid under Ames Code Annotated 38-17-1034, two witnesses must attest that they saw the testator sign the will in their presence. In this case, one witness watched the testator sign the will. A second witness was taking a call in an adjoining office. She didn't see the testator sign the will, but she saw the signature on the page moments later. The trial court ruled that the

will was invalid because the will was not signed in the presence of the second witness.

Legal Principle: ______________________________

Key Facts: ______________________________

Question: ______________________________

Bonus example:

Remember this brain breaker from several pages ago?

Whether the Prosecution improperly severed two counts involving the exact same conduct (in this matter, one count of "Especially Aggravated Robbery" and one count of "Aggravated Kidnapping") in two separate indictments despite the fact that they should have been joined under mandatory joinder under Tennessee Rules of Criminal Procedure Rule 8(a), is the Prosecution obligated to dismiss the non-joined charge ("Aggravated Kidnapping") prior to the Defendant's trial for "Especially Aggravated Robbery" to avoid tainting the Defendant's trial in that evidence of the second charge (for which the Defendant had not yet been tried for) with unfair prejudice, thus denying the Defendant's right to a fair and impartial trial under the U.S. and Tennessee Constitutions?

The alternative might be something like this:

Joinder is mandatory if the offenses are based on the same conduct or arise from the same criminal episode, within the jurisdiction of a single court, and known to the appropriate prosecuting official at the time of the return of the indictment. Here, the Prosecution charged the Defendant with Aggravated Robbery and Aggravated Kidnapping in two separate indictments even though they were based on the same conduct. Did the trial court err in denying the Defendant's motion to dismiss?

And One More Thing

If nothing else, this chapter should show the importance of preserving, raising, and phrasing the issues you want the court to review. With enough time and effort, you will make a strong impression on any reader who flips first to this page of the brief.

More importantly, if you put the time and effort into phrasing the issue and your opponent doesn't, you will frame the terms of the debate.

CHAPTER VI

Summary of the Argument

The Summary of the Argument is a sneak preview of the strongest arguments you intend to make. Imagine that it's the only part of the brief the court will read. Here are three things to consider.[1] First, focus on only two or three points. If you have multiple issues, focus on the two or three strongest. You may have a LOT more reasons in your brief. But the summary of the argument is just that: a summary. Think of it like this. If someone were to ask you to name your favorite movies, you'd tell them two or three. Because no one, not even your best friend, will remember your fourteen favorite movies.

Second, connect the appeal to a larger theme. We talked about the theme as part of storytelling, and that's often a great way to capture the court's attention here as well. Here are some examples:

[1] In the brief, the summary of the argument comes before the argument, and it may be difficult to summarize something until you know what it is you are summarizing. (I realize I just used summary, summarize, and summarizing in the same sentence, but it made sense in my head.) So, you should hold off on writing the summary of the argument until after you've written the argument. In fact, feel free to just skim this chapter as long as you promise to come back.

- This case involves key issues of first impression.
- This case raises important constitutional questions.
- John Wayne Slate stands convicted of a crime he did not commit.
- Like all other teenagers convicted of first-degree murder in Tennessee, Joe Doe was automatically sentenced to life imprisonment with no consideration of his age and no chance for parole for over sixty years.
- The plaintiff was one of thousands of victims who lost their life savings after relying on the defendant for truthful and accurate advice.

Third, think about the relief you want. In a narrow sense, you may want the court to reverse and remand for a new trial. Or you may want the court to vacate the judgment and dismiss. Or you may want the court to affirm the grant of summary judgment. And so on. But be creative. In a broader sense, you might want the court to correct a miscarriage of justice. Or you may want the court to put an end to an unfair practice. Or reinforce constitutional protections. Or stand by established precedent. Or apply the plain meaning of the applicable statute. You get the idea.

Let's see how these three ideas come together.

Example 1

This example begins with a subtle but effective emotional hook. Although you should avoid making a blatant emotional appeal to an appellate court, it's hard to be too cynical about a case involving an injured child. The rest of the summary makes three key points with the simplest of roadmaps: "first, second, and finally." If you were making these points to someone in a conversation, you might even count each point on your fingers as you go along.

SUMMARY OF THE ARGUMENT

David and Laurie Miller brought this action after their two-year-old child Amber received a vaccination manufactured by Respondent and suffered extensive and permanent injuries.

The district court dismissed the action under section 22(b)(1) of the National Childhood Vaccine Injury Act, which expressly precludes design defect claims against vaccine manufacturers only for "unavoidable" side effects caused by vaccines covered under the statute. et seq. Because the plain language of the statute, sound public policy, and the specific facts of this case militate against preemption of all design defect claims under section 22(b)(1), this Court must reverse the trial court's ruling.

First, the plain language of section 22(b)(1) limits the preemption of design defect claims to those based upon side effects which are unavoidable despite proper manufacturing and labeling. Design defect claims predicated upon avoidable side effects despite proper manufacturing and labeling are not preempted by section 22(b)(1). Indeed, broad preemption of all design defect claims would eliminate compensation for vaccine-injury victims in direct contravention of Congress's clear and manifest purpose to provide sufficient compensation for such victims under the Vaccine Act. Had Congress intended for such a drastic result, it would have simply said so in the statute.

Second, allowing section 22(b)(1) to create unlimited tort immunity from design defect claims for vaccine manufacturers undermines a strong state interest in compensating the victims of defectively manufactured products. While no doubt profitable for Respondent and like manufacturers, such broad immunity would be unsupported by the statute and conflict with sound public policy. Not surprisingly, not a single decision has adopted such a theory.

Finally, although Respondent asserts that Amber's injuries were unavoidable, the record is replete with examples of feasible alternative designs. As a result, genuine issues of material fact exist as to whether Respondent had a feasible alternative design of the vaccine available and whether the injuries were unavoidable. This Court must overturn the summary judgment and remand for further proceedings.

Example 2

This example involves a constitutional issue of first impression. Hopefully that's *two* reasons the court should pay attention. And the summary contains two key points: "The use of a drone was an unlawful search; and even if the drone was not an unlawful search, the face print was unlawfully obtained." Notice the "heads we win, tails they lose" technique.

SUMMARY OF THE ARGUMENT

This case presents an issue of first impression: whether the Government's use of a camera mounted to a military-style drone to obtain a face print of an individual from within his curtilage, and the subsequent analysis of the face print, amounts to a search and seizure under the Fourth Amendment.

The Fourth Amendment guarantees the right of the people to be secure in their homes and persons against unreasonable searches and seizures. A search and seizure is presumptively unreasonable when conducted without a warrant. Accordingly, because the governmental surveillance in this case did indeed amount to a search and seizure, it was unreasonable in violation of Dr. Stephenson's Fourth Amendment rights.

Governmental conduct amounts to a search where it invades an area that is entitled to a reasonable expectation of privacy. A reasonable expectation of privacy exists when an individual has a subjective expectation of privacy that society is willing to recognize as reasonable. As applied specifically to sense-enhancing technology, the government's use of technology is a search where it uses a technology that is not in general public use to obtain intimate information from an area that is entitled to an expectation of privacy.

Here, the government's conduct amounted to a search because it used two technologies that are not in general public use—a military-style drone and a biometric facial recognition technology camera—to obtain Dr. Stephenson's face print from him while he stood within his curtilage, an area that is entitled to a heightened expectation of privacy.

But even if obtaining the image itself did not amount to a search, the collection and subsequent analysis of Dr. Stephenson's face print did. This court has routinely held that the collection and testing of physiological data, such as DNA samples and urine samples, is a search and seizure because these procedures identify the individual and obtain private information.

For these reasons, the court must reverse the convictions.

Example 3

In addition or instead of making your points, consider refuting the opposing side or lower court. Notice how this example sets 'em up and then knocks 'em down.

> **SUMMARY OF ARGUMENT**
>
> Defendant asserts that the statute at issue did not provide fair warning that his conduct was illegal. As the trial court correctly noted, the Defendant cited no authority for this proposition. Defendant also claims that the district court erred in denying his request to provide funds for an expert witness. But he did not file his motion timely, nor did he make a particularized showing in support of his request. Finally, he claims that the district court erred in denying his motion for a judgment of acquittal. But as the district court found, the evidence of guilt was sufficient, indeed overwhelming. This Court must affirm the judgment below.

Example 4

This example begins with the theme before addressing each part of a three-part test.

> The Plaintiff's attempt to create a right of publicity where one does not exist should be rejected Because its risks extinguishing the creative freedom that every citizen enjoys under the First Amendment.
>
> As the district court found, the Defendant used a default avatar consisting of a non-literal depiction of the Plaintiff's likeness and biographical information that was publicly available. Second, the Defendant placed its default avatar in an entirely different context from which the Plaintiff normally exists. Finally, the Defendant

included an extensive avatar-altering feature, which allowed and encouraged users to modify the default avatar. For these reasons, this court should affirm the district court's judgment.

And One More Thing

Remember that the summary should be written after the bulk of the argument section has been drafted. That's when you'll know the issues and the key arguments underlying those issues. As these examples show, that's also when you may develop broader themes and ideas that tie everything together.

If you're having trouble deciding what to include in the summary of the argument, think of how this section relates to an oral argument. Let's say you have fifteen minutes. What issues would you present to the court? What result do you want the court to reach? What two or three points would lead the court to that result? The clock is ticking, so you must be concise. When viewed through this lens, you'll know exactly what to include in the summary.

PART THREE

The Argument

CHAPTER VII

The Argument: Structure

Now that you have the readers' attention, it's time for the argument. Wait, let's try that again. Now that you have the readers' attention, it's time for. . .

The Argument.

That's better. This is where you interpret and apply legal principles. This is where you must be compelling and persuasive. This is where you must be organized and clear. This is where you win or lose. This is your opportunity to overcome the odds we discussed at the very beginning.[1]

If that sounded a little dramatic, don't worry. We just need to start with the three basic skills you've been developing since the first semester of law school.

1. *Legal research.* Using all means at your disposal, find the primary and secondary authorities relating to the issues raised in the brief. There's no way around this fundamental task.

---

[1] This is where I start a sentence with "this is" for the last time.

2. *Legal interpretation.* Take the time to make sense of the legal research. Very often this means reading statutes, regulations, and constitutional provisions. And it nearly always means reading a bunch of court decisions.

3. *Legal reasoning.* Apply the legal principles to the facts in the record of your case, compare your case to other cases, and refute opposing arguments.

As you know, the above three steps never really end. Sources cite more sources. Interpreting authority leads to more research. Applying legal principles leads to roadblocks that require more research, interpretation, and analysis. In short, legal analysis is not a linear process from A to B to C; it's more like a looping process from A to B back to A then to C and then, oops, back to B and then, aww man, all the way back to A and *then, thank goodness,* back to C, etc.

Suffice to say, following this process for every issue in the brief generates a lot of content, as the internet would say. (That's right, I just quoted the internet). Rather than rush to the keyboard and hope for inspiration to strike, take a few minutes, a few hours, or a few days to gather your thoughts. You might create a formal outline or take notes on your computer or a legal pad. Any form of brainstorming or planning will do. Before it became this ~~polished~~, ~~erudite~~, *dazzling* contribution to the *Short and Happy* series, much of this guide was scribbled on notebook paper and Post-it notes.

A. Standard CREAC (Pronounced "Cree-ack")

When it comes to getting all that content on the page, think about that strange device you may have learned in your first semester: CREAC. A well-structured CREAC does the following:

- Begins with the conclusion ("C") the court should reach, often stated as a point heading or thesis sentence. (Hold that thought.)
- Identifies and interprets the legal principles or rules ("R") governing a key issue, whether they stem from constitutions, statutes, or case law. (That's why you did all the research and interpretation.)
- Uses examples ("E") to show how the same legal principles have been applied in other cases. (That's why precedent matters.)
- Shows the court how the legal principles and examples apply ("A") to the facts of the case. (That is your legal reasoning.)
- Ends with the conclusion ("C") the court should reach. (You know, just in case the reader missed it the first time.)

You might have learned that CREAC also goes by the name of CRAC. And its other aliases include TREAC, TRAC, and IRAC. (The "T" is for "thesis," the "I" is for issue, and everything else is pretty much the same.)[2]

Do these devices seem a little odd? Sure. Do they seem a little rigid? Maybe. Do they work when it comes to getting material on the page? The *Short and Happy* answer is, "Yes, they sure do."

Example 1

Here's a basic CREAC used in a constitutional case. (My comments are in italics before each component.)

---

[2] In case you're wondering, the various devices are pronounced See-rack, Tree-rack, Tee-rack, and Eye-rack. Where else could you go for this kind of quality instruction?

This CREAC begins with a point heading or thesis statement that states the conclusion the court should reach. A good point heading, like this one, contains a legal principle and a few key facts.

The Government Violated Mr. Wilson's Fourth Amendment Rights When It Installed A Surveillance Camera Outside His Home Without A Warrant.

After the point heading, the "R" in this CREAC begins with the Fourth Amendment. Although "R" stands for rules, it might also stand for research because that's what goes here.

> The Fourth Amendment guarantees individuals the "right [ ] to be secure in their persons, houses, papers, and effects, against unreasonable searches and seizures" and states that "no Warrants shall issue, but upon probable cause, supported by Oath or affirmation, and particularly describing the place to be searched, and the persons or things to be seized." U.S. Const. amend. IV.

Now that readers know the relevant constitutional language, the next portion of the "R" section uses more specific legal principles to remind the reader when a search has occurred. Notice that synthesizing legal principles creates a "general to specific" roadmap.

> A search occurs within the meaning of the Fourth Amendment when the Government obtains information by either (1) physically trespassing upon private property or (2) intruding upon a sphere where an individual has a reasonable expectation of privacy. *See Carpenter v. United States*, 585 U.S. 296, 304 (2018).

These legal principles will now focus on homes and curtilage.

> The Fourth Amendment provides the most protection to the home and the curtilage: "the area 'immediately

surrounding and associated with the home.' " *Florida v. Jardines*, 569 U.S. 1, 6 (2013) (quoting *Oliver v. United States*, 466 U.S. 170, 180 (1984)). "At the Amendment's 'very core' stands 'the right of a man to retreat into his own home and there be free from unreasonable governmental intrusion.' " *Jardines*, 569 U.S. at 6 (quoting *Silverman v. United States*, 365 U.S. 505, 511 (1961)). "To give full practical effect to that right, the Court considers curtilage . . . to be 'part of the home itself for Fourth Amendment purposes.'" *Jardines*, 569 U. S. at 6. "The protection afforded the curtilage is essentially a protection of families and personal privacy in an area intimately linked to the home, both physically and psychologically, where privacy expectations are most heightened." *California v. Ciraolo*, 476 U.S. 207, 212-13 (1986).

To continue narrowing the focus, the reader will be shown several examples ("E") in which courts have handled similar cases. Why do prior cases matter? That's right, the doctrine of stare decisis.

Long-term, continuous video surveillance of a home raises an equally, if not more, severe intrusion into the privacies of life than that of location data. For example Fourth Amendment principles dictate that eight-month video surveillance of the defendant's curtilage constituted a search. *United States v. Moore-Bush*, 381 F. Supp. 3d 139, 150 (D. Mass. 2019). Similarly, continuous and covert recording of a defendant's home for six weeks violated an expectation of privacy. *Shafer v. City of Boulder*, 896 F. Supp. 2d 915, 918 (D. Nev. 2012) (holding that continuous video surveillance of defendant's backyard violated the Fourth Amendment). Likewise, , the warrantless use of a pole camera, specifically

> installed to chronicle and observe the accused's activities outside his residence. . . constituted a search under the Fourth Amendment." *South Dakota v. Jones*, 903 N.W.2d 101, 113 (S.D. 2017)The court emphasized that "its use violates an expectation of privacy that society is prepared to recognize as reasonable."

Whew. Look at what's been done so far. You have shared your conclusion, legal principles, and examples with the reader. That's the CRE of the CREAC. What's next? That's right, applying the principles and examples in the "A" of the CREAC. And let's face it, this section is what the judges are really waiting for. Notice the word "here" is used as the key transition:

> Here, the recording was obtained in violation of Mr. Wilson's reasonable expectation of privacy. The recording captured all types of intimate details focused on the home at 616 Atlantic Avenue. The officers saw which individuals came and went from the home. They enhanced the video to capture license plate numbers of guests. They identified when the home was used for political organizing, who attended, and how long they stayed. Officers recognized frequent visitors and infrequent visitors. They determined who stayed overnight. They saw personal items people carried in and out, which cars items came from, and in which cars items left.
>
> This continued for ten months, twenty-four hours a day. The Government essentially argues it is entitled—without any measure of suspicion or judicial oversight—to record the intimate details of every American citizen's life at the footsteps of her private retreat. No court has allowed that to happen.

Finally, don't forget to re-state your conclusion ("C").

In short, this Court must reverse the judgment and dismiss the conviction.

As this example reveals, the CREAC device simply allows a reader to follow the legal analysis one step at a time: General legal principles, specific legal principles, case examples, and application of those legal principles and examples. That's how we are taught to analyze legal issues from day one of law school. And that's how judges evaluate your arguments when deciding cases.

B. CREACs and creacs

The CREAC structure is especially useful when breaking your argument into smaller parts. In most cases, the legal principles consist of multiple statutory elements or a series of factors gleaned from case law. Some cases simply throw up their hands and give us a good, old-fashioned totality of circumstances test.

In these cases, the CREAC structure can be broken into an overview or umbrella section followed by a series of CREACS that address one element or factor at a time. In fact, you may think of the smaller parts as "creacs." Because that sounds ridiculous, let's walk through another example. For the sake of brevity, I will summarize or omit some of the authority to focus on the larger structure and not the substantive content. (You're welcome.) Okay, ready? Here we go. *As in the previous example, the argument begins with a point heading that informs the court what conclusion ("C") to reach.*

I. The Evidence was Insufficient Because No Rational Trier of Fact Could Find the Elements of First-Degree Murder Beyond a Reasonable Doubt

Like most criminal offenses, first degree murder is governed by statute. Whenever your legal analysis stems from a statute, you can often begin your rule ("R") section right there. Because this statute contains all of the elements of first-degree murder, this first paragraph serves as an overview. Like this:

> As charged in this case, first-degree murder includes the intentional and premeditated killing of another person. Tenn. Code Ann. § 39-13-204. Neither element was proven in this case.

Now watch this. Because the overview told the reader that first-degree murder has two elements, the analysis now turns to the first element. Because this sub-point heading is the conclusion about intent as the first of two elements, you might think of it as (c) instead of (C).

The evidence was insufficient to show the defendant acted intentionally.

Next, the reader is given legal principles or rules about the element "intent." Think of these as the "r" for this creac. That definition is found in a statute as well.

> A person acts intentionally "with respect to the nature of the conduct or to a result of the conduct when it is the person's conscious objective or desire to engage in the conduct or cause the result." Tenn. Code Ann. § 39-11-106(21).

What comes next? That's right. Any cases that serve as examples with respect to the element of intent. Think of this as the "e" of this creac. I'm going to abbreviate those discussions to keep these examples short and happy.

> Several courts have reversed first-degree murder convictions where the proof failed to establish that a defendant acted intentionally. Brief discussion of case A followed by a brief discussion of case B and so on.

Next, the analysis applies the principles and examples about intent to the evidence in our case. Let's call that (a).

> Here, no reasonable trier of fact could find evidence of intent beyond a reasonable doubt because blah blah blah. This case is like cases A and B for the following reasons and so on. . . .

Now, the analysis concludes with regard to the element of intent:

> Because the evidence of intent was insufficient, this Court must reverse the conviction for first-degree murder.

Now watch what happens. Having disposed of the first element of first-degree murder (intent), the example turns to the second element (premeditation). In the following passages, you will see the conclusion, rules, examples, and application relating solely to this element.

> **In addition, the evidence was insufficient to show the defendant acted with premeditation.**
>
> Premeditation "is an act done after the exercise of reflection and judgment." Although "the intent to kill must have been formed prior to the act itself," it is not necessary "that the purpose to kill preexist in the mind of the accused for any definite period of time." Tenn. Code Ann. § 39-11-202(e).
>
> Several courts have said that premeditation is established by evidence that a defendant threatened to kill the victim in advance of the offense, took steps to obtain a weapon, and waited in hiding for the victim to appear. Discuss Case C and Case D.
>
> Here, the evidence presented by the State was insufficient to support premeditation, etc. Discuss the

facts and the absence of evidence. Compare this case to cases C and D.

Because the evidence of premeditation was insufficient, this Court should reverse the conviction for first-degree murder.

Now, having addressed intent and premeditation as separate elements (with separate creacs) the analysis must connect the dots by wrapping up first-degree murder as a whole.

Because the evidence did not support either element of first-degree murder, this Court must reverse and dismiss the conviction.

When viewed in this way, you can see that the analysis had a CREAC for first-degree murder. That CREAC for first-degree murder consisted of a little creac for intent and a little creac for premeditation. I mean, c'mon. How adorable are little creacs, right? Like little nesting Santas.

The same ideas work when you have several factors under case law. Let's say you have an issue involving the establishment clause under the First Amendment based on a School Board's prayer practice. The traditional *Lemon* analysis has three parts: secular purpose, secular effect, and excessive entanglement. You would create a large CREAC for whether the School Board's practice violates the establishment clause. But that CREAC could analyze one part at a time with little creacs. Something like this.

First, begin with the conclusion.

I. The School Board's prayer did not amount to the establishment of a religion under the Supreme Court's three-part *Lemon* analysis.

Next, provide an overview with a discussion of the first amendment, the establishment clause, and the Lemon test. Telling the reader that Lemon has three factors indicates that they may be addressed one at a time. You would then build creacs around the following sub-point headings.

A. The prayer practice serves to solemnize School Board meetings and therefore has a secular purpose.

B. Since the School Board's prayer practice has the principal and primary effect of solemnizing meetings, favors neither religion nor non-religion, and is effectuated by students and not parochial teachers, it neither advances nor inhibits religion.

C. The School Board's prayer practice does not foster an excessive government entanglement with religion because the School Board need not maintain surveillance over the practice and the prayer practice does not require specific government oversight.

By addressing each factor separately, the task becomes more manageable for the reader. And for you. Everything you researched, interpreted, and applied has a place to go on the page. It's a bit like working on a puzzle. The CREAC itself is like the outside edges of the puzzle, and that's what you build first. The content consists of the inside puzzle pieces.

And here's another thing to keep in mind. Whenever you break a large issue—whether there was a search, whether the evidence established first degree murder, or whether school board prayer violated the establishment clause—into smaller parts, you will likely find that your arguments on some factors or elements are stronger than others. It's unlikely that your analysis of each element or factor will be of equal strength. So, you can shape your arguments with that in mind. The reader will appreciate you for breaking something large into smaller bits; they may even appreciate you for conceding that some parts of your arguments are stronger than others. That's also a great way to establish credibility with the court.

That's huge.

C. Adding Rebuttal

As explained above, the CREAC structure allows you to get legal research, interpretation, and reasoning onto the page in a way that other lawyers and judges can follow. Focus on using the strongest authority and making your strongest arguments. That includes addressing and rebutting opposing arguments.

Here's the "A" paragraph we looked at earlier, this time adding and emphasizing the responses to opposing arguments in bold:

> Here, the recording was obtained in violation of Mr. Wilson's reasonable expectation of privacy. The recording captured all types of intimate details focused on the home at 616 Atlantic Avenue. The officers saw which individuals came and went from the home. They enhanced the video to capture license plate numbers of guests. They identified when the home was used for political organizing, who attended, and how long they stayed. Officers recognized frequent visitors and infrequent visitors. They determined who stayed overnight. They saw personal items people carried in and out, which cars items came from, and in which cars items left.
>
> **Although the Government cites *United States v. Morgan*, that case involved a federal agent who passed by a defendant's home on only a few occasions. That case has little to do with the use of video surveillance month after month. Put simply, the Government argues it is entitled—without any measure of suspicion or**

judicial oversight—to record the intimate details of every American citizen's life. This cannot stand.

What's more, the Government's position is simply not supported by the record. No witness testified A, B, and C as the Government's brief suggests. To the contrary, nearly every witness claimed X, Y, and Z.

And so on.

In short, your analysis is not complete until you have addressed and refuted the opposing arguments, including the reasoning of a lower court. As the above example shows, that means dealing with and distinguishing any cases the opposing party or lower court relied on. We will discuss these ideas in more depth a bit later in this guide.

D. Adding Facts

In some cases, the analysis may need a factual or procedural background between the point heading (C) and the rules (R). This is particularly useful in complex cases or cases with facts that don't entirely fit into the statement of the facts. For example, an issue about expert testimony may need the reader to know details from exhibits or an evidentiary hearing. Likewise, a suppression issue may need the reader to know the contents of a search warrant or the testimony presented in a suppression hearing. Even if you touched on those topics in your statement of facts, the reader could use a bit more context before getting into the argument.

To that end, create a point heading as always and immediately provide an overview of the facts regarding that specific issue. With that factual context in place, you can turn to the legal principles and analysis. Like this:

The Trial Court Erred in Denying the Motion to Suppress Where Officers' Warrantless Search of the Defendant's Home Was Not Supported by Exigent Circumstances.

After this conclusion, summarize the testimony and evidence that was presented at the suppression hearing, as well as the trial court's factual findings and conclusions. As always, cite to the record. Make sure readers have all the information they need before getting into the legal analysis. This may consist of a few sentences, a few paragraphs or even a few pages. But after that material is in place, the reader is prepared to dive into the rules, examples and application.

At this point, you may be thinking, "Hey, Barckhoff, would adding facts to a traditional CREAC make that a CFREAC?" Yes. Yes, it would. "Could we pronounce it See-Freak?" We absolutely can. Now you're getting the hang of things.

And One More Thing

The CREAC and similar structures allow you to get your research and analysis onto the page in a way the reader can follow. And once the material is on the page, you can and should consider even more ways to convey your arguments.[3] In fact, think of CREAC as the major scale in music; once you learn that, you can make any changes you might like. (If you're keeping track, I've now compared CREAC to playing the major scale and assembling a puzzle.)

[3] *See generally* Diane B. Kraft, *CREAC in the Real World*, 63 Clev. St. L. Rev. 567 (2015).

CHAPTER VIII

The Argument: "Result"

Now that we've reviewed CREAC and its variations, it's time to delve into the argument in more detail. An effective and persuasive argument needs to answer three questions: what result do you want, how can the court reach that result, and why should the court reach that result.

Let's start with the result. Everything in an appellate brief should point to the result you want. That's especially true in a CREAC because it begins and ends with the conclusion. Be as clear as possible as often as possible. Do not give the court an opportunity to write a decision that says something like this: "The appellant *appears* to be asking such and such." Or worse, "The appellant has not identified the relief sought." Yep, they'll do that.

A. Drafting Point Headings

As we discussed in the last chapter, the opening "C" in a CREAC is a point heading that combines a legal principle with key facts. The point heading must be clear and concise. Hmmm. Does that sound familiar?

Yep, we did the same exercise when drafting the statement of the issues. Consider this issue:

> *Whether* this Court Must Affirm the Defendant's Conviction for Federal Bank Robbery Where the Defendant Used Force to Take Money Withdrawn From an ATM.

Now watch this:

> This Court Must Affirm the Defendant's Conviction for Federal Bank Robbery Because the Defendant Used Force to Take Money Withdrawn from an ATM.

See the relation? A difference of just two words.

The issue presented at the beginning of a brief mirrors a point heading in the argument of the brief. Therefore, we should be wary of some of the same things. We don't want a point heading that has too little:

- The Trial Court Erred.
- The Fourth Amendment Issue.
- The *Lemon* Test.
- Element One: Premeditation.
- Whether the evidence was admissible.
- The Trial Court Erred in Denying the Motion to Suppress.
- The Trial Court Correctly Granted Summary Judgment.
- This court should reverse.

Or too much:

> The Court of Appeals erred in concluding that the testimony of an expert witness was not testimonial under

Crawford and its progeny and thereby affirming the judgment of the trial court denying the motion in limine seeking to exclude the testimony under the Fifth Amendment to the United States and Article I, section 8 of the Tennessee Constitution.

Let's see how that works with the issues we examined earlier in this guide.

Example 1

Issue:

Whether a [confession was voluntary under the 5th and 14th amendments] where [the defendant was questioned for four days, denied food and water, and beaten with barbed wire.]

Point Heading:

The Defendant's confession was involuntary under the 5th and 14th amendments because he was questioned for four days, denied food and water, and beaten with barbed wire.

Example 2

Issue:

Whether [the trial court correctly awarded a divorce and alimony to Wife] where [Husband was physically abusive, emotionally cruel, and a serial adulterer].

Point Hearing:

The trial court correctly granted a divorce and alimony to Wife after finding that Husband was physically abusive, emotionally cruel, and a serial adulterer.

Example 3

Issue:

Whether [testimony was admissible as an excited utterance under Fed. R. Evid. 803] where [the declarant saw a man wearing a hockey mask and holding a chainsaw and immediately shouted, "That looks like the defendant; let's hide in the cemetery!"]

Point Heading:

The trial court correctly admitted a statement as an excited utterance under Rule 803 where a declarant who saw a man wearing a hockey mask and holding a chainsaw and immediately shouted, "That looks like the defendant; let's hide in the cemetery!"

Example 4

Issue:

Whether [the employer violated Title VI or Title VII] where [employee was fired for reporting senior management's culture of drug use and sexual harassment].

Point Heading:

This Court should reverse summary judgment for the Defendant where material issues of fact exist about whether the employee was fired in retaliation for reporting senior management's culture of drug use and sexual harassment.

Pretty cool, huh? The time and effort you spent in drafting the issues presented creates a thread throughout the entire argument.

B. Organizing Point Headings (and Sub-Point Headings)

Once you get a handle on *phrasing* point headings, make an impact with the way you *use* them. As far back as the table of contents, we talked about how point headings and subheadings reveal your structure and analysis. The connection should be clearer now.

Pop quiz.

On a scale of one to ten, with one being mind-numbing and ten being mind-blowing, evaluate the following point headings and subpoint headings:

Example 1

I. The District Court Properly Granted Summary Judgment for the Government in this Section 1983 Action.

   A. Liberty interest.

   B. Balancing test.

II. Summary Judgment Was Proper Because the Plaintiff did not establish grounds for relief under the Eighth Amendment.

   A. Substantial risk of significant harm.

   B. Deliberate indifference.

Meh? Now compare that with ***Example 2:***

I. The District Court Properly Granted Summary Judgment for the Government in this Section 1983 Action Because Assigning the Plaintiff to Administrative Segregation for Capital Murder Did Not Violate the Fourteenth Amendment.

A. Plaintiff did not establish a state created liberty interest because his assignment to administrative segregation did not impose an atypical and significant hardship compared to ordinary solitary confinement.

B. Even if Plaintiff established a liberty interest, his interest in avoiding administrative segregation is substantially outweighed by the Government's interest in keeping death-sentenced inmates separate from the prison population.

II. The District Court Properly Granted Summary Judgment for the Government in this Section 1983 Action Because Assigning the Plaintiff to Administrative Segregation For Capital Murder Did Not Violate the Eighth Amendment.

A. The conditions of Plaintiff's confinement do not pose a substantial risk of significant harm because he has all of life's necessities, receives medical attention, and does not suffer from the wanton infliction of pain.

B. Even if a substantial risk of significant harm exists, there was no evidence that prison officials were deliberately indifferent to the harm.

Ah-ha! Even if your mind wasn't blown, did you score the second one higher? What did you notice? More content, that's for sure. But what else?

- Point headings I and II are conclusions.
- Point headings I and II are consistently phrased.

- Point headings I and II tell the court what conclusion to reach.
- Point headings I and II break the analysis into two parts.

But wait, there's more:

- Sub-point headings "A" and "B" are also conclusions.
- Sub-point headings "A" and "B" have a logical relationship: even if our conclusion about A is wrong, our conclusion about B is correct.

Also note, of course, that subheadings A and B are conclusions that set up the CREACs on those issues. Here's another example to rate on the mind-numbing v. mind blowing meter:

I. The trial court properly granted summary judgment where the Defendants violated the Plaintiff's son's freedom of speech under the First Amendment.

  A. Plaintiff's son's speech was not connected to the school.

  B. Plaintiff's son's speech did not cause any material or foreseeable disruption to school.

Once again, these well-developed headings include the type of case, a few facts about the case, the conclusions the party seeks, and roadmaps for how to reach that conclusion. You can already predict how the analysis will be developed from subheadings A and B with CREACs or some variation.

Not bad from a bunch of point headings.

C. Other Opportunities to Show the Result

In addition to the point headings, a brief offers several more opportunities to make the result unmistakable.

1. *Relief Sought*

A brief must conclude by "stating the precise relief sought."[1] But you don't need to keep the reader in suspense by waiting until the very end.

2. *Applying the Standard of Review*

When incorporating the standard of review, remind the court how that affects the result. That often works at the end of the argument, the end of a CREAC, and so on. Some examples:

- Because the trial court abused its discretion, this court must reverse the judgment and remand for a new trial.
- As a result, this court should reverse because the trial court's findings were clearly erroneous.
- Because the appellant failed to show that the trial court abused its discretion, this Court must simply affirm.
- Simply put, no rational trier of fact could find the elements beyond a reasonable doubt. This court must dismiss the conviction.
- Because the trial court's error more likely than not affected the outcome, this court must reverse and remand for a new trial.
- Because the trial court's ruling was harmless beyond a reasonable doubt, this court must affirm.

---

[1] Fed. R. App. P. 28(a)(9).

3. *Summary of Argument*

As we discussed earlier, the summary of the argument includes the theme of the case and the key arguments that will be made. The summary should conclude by telling the court exactly what result to reach: affirm, reverse, dismiss, or remand for further proceedings.

> ***And One More Thing***
>
> Getting the result you want means the client gets relief. Always keep that in mind. Without getting relief for your client, the appeal is academic. (And not in a good way.)

CHAPTER IX

The Argument: "Roadmap"

It's one thing to tell the court what result you want. It's another to show the court how to arrive at that result. Think of this as giving the court a roadmap. Or think of this as the R and E in a CREAC. Regardless, courts expect lawyers to explain and synthesize legal principles cogently and concisely. Courts do not want lawyers to copy and paste long passages into a brief. And they definitely don't want forms of artificial intelligence to do that, either. Let's take a closer look at the techniques and challenges when trying to put the law on the page.

A. Synthesize Legal Principles: General to Specific

When creating a legal roadmap, remember to start with general principles and work toward specific examples. If you glance back at earlier chapters, especially the chapter about CREAC, you'll notice that our passages had that in common.

1. Constitutional Issues

For a constitutional issue, the roadmap often follows this general course:

Constitutional provision

↓

Purpose stated in case law or secondary sources

↓

Relevant material found in historical sources

↓

Controlling and persuasive case law examples

2. Statutory Issues

For a case governed primarily by statutory or regulatory provisions, the roadmap looks more like this:

Statutory scheme and purpose

↓

Specific statutory provisions and language

↓

Statutory elements and definitions

↓

Controlling and persuasive case law examples

3. Common law issues

For issues governed principally by case law, it's more of the same:

Case law claims or defenses

↓

Factors or tests synthesized from case law

↓

Controlling and persuasive case law examples

B. Use Your Own Words

Organizing material from general to specific *always* works. It's like googling an image of the earth, and then zooming in on a particular country, state, city, street, and house. (And that, my friends, is a sentence that I would never have expected to write when I was in law school.)

But that's not enough. A solid roadmap should guide the reader through the material. It's not enough to copy and paste "the law" onto the page. (Or worse, allow AI to do that for you.) You must also synthesize the material. In your own words.

Example 1

This passage contains legal principles using the "general to specific" approach. But it's the phrases in bold that stitch the principles together.

> ***The Eighth Amendment protects inmates against*** **"cruel and unusual punishments."** US. Const. Amend. 8. ***This provision prohibits only*** "the wanton and unnecessary infliction of pain," ***as well as punishments that are*** "grossly disproportionate to the severity of the

> crime warranting imprisonment." *Rhodes v. Chapman*, 452 U.S. 337, 349 (1981). ***For example, prison officials must ensure that inmates*** "receive adequate food, clothing, shelter, and medical care." Id. ***Prison officials must also*** "take reasonable measures to guarantee the safety of the inmates." *Farmer v. Brennan*, 511 U.S. 825, 832 (1994). ***But*** "[t]he Constitution 'does not mandate comfortable prisons,' " ***only* "humane" ones**. *Hudson v. Palmer*, 468 U.S. 517, 526-27 (1984)).

Example 2

Like example 1, this excerpt begins with a constitutional principle that leads to an exception that leads to specific cases. The connecting language in bold italics makes the passage much easier to follow than would a series of copied and pasted quotes.

> ***Although the Fifth Amendment provides that no person*** "shall be compelled in any criminal case to be a witness against himself," ***the protections apply only when a person is*** "compelled to make a testimonial statement that is incriminating." U.S. CONST. amend. V.; *Fisher v. United States*, 425 U.S. 391, 408 (1976). ***For example, courts have consistently held that the Fifth Amendment is not implicated when the foregone conclusion exception applies***. *Fisher*, 425 U.S. at 408.
>
> ***The foregone conclusion exception applies if*** "at the time [the Government] sought the act of production, it knew with 'reasonable particularity' that (1) the evidence existed; (2) the evidence was in the defendant's possession or control; and (3) the evidence was authentic." *United States v. Hubbell*, 530 U.S. 27, 40-41 (2000). In *State v. Andrews*, 234 A.3d 2354, 1266 (N.J. 2020), ***for example, the court concluded that the*** "Fifth Amendment's Self-Incrimination Clause [did] not protect

[the defendant] from government compelled disclosure of a cell phone passcode."

C. Statutory Roadmaps

Constructing a statutory roadmap presents more challenges. In fact, nothing tells the court "Good luck with that" quite like copying and pasting an entire statute into your brief. Let's look at some examples.

Example 1

Imagine reading a case about first-degree murder and finding that the brief has simply copied and pasted the following statutory material.

First degree murder is as follows:

(a) First degree murder is:

(1) A premeditated and intentional killing of another;

(2) A killing of another committed in the perpetration of or attempt to perpetrate any first degree murder, act of terrorism, arson, rape, robbery, burglary, theft, kidnapping, physical abuse in violation of § 71-6-119, aggravated neglect of an elderly or vulnerable adult in violation of § 39-15-508, aggravated child abuse, aggravated child neglect, rape of a child, aggravated rape of a child or aircraft piracy; or

(3) A killing of another committed as the result of the unlawful throwing, placing or discharging of a destructive device or bomb.

(b) No culpable mental state is required for conviction under subdivision (a)(2) or (a)(3), except the intent to commit the enumerated offenses or acts in those subdivisions.

(c) A person convicted of first degree murder shall be punished by:

1. Death;

2. Imprisonment for life without possibility of parole; or

3. Imprisonment for life.

(d) As used in subdivision (a)(1), "premeditation" is an act done after the exercise of reflection and judgment. "Premeditation" means that the intent to kill must have been formed prior to the act itself. It is not necessary that the purpose to kill preexist in the mind of the accused for any definite period of time. The mental state of the accused at the time the accused allegedly decided to kill must be carefully considered in order to determine whether the accused was sufficiently free from excitement and passion as to be capable of premeditation.

Tenn. Code Ann. 39-13-202(a)-(d).

Sure, it's all interesting and certainly comprehensive. But is it easy to read? And does it give the reader any sense of direction? What part of the statute will have relevance? There's no way to know.

Example 2

In contrast, this example interprets the statute and guides the reader through the relevant provisions.

> ***In Tennessee, first degree murder requires an*** "intentional and premeditated killing of another person." Tenn. Code Ann. 39-13-202(a)(1). ***An act is intentional when it is a*** "person's conscious objective or desire to engage in the conduct or cause the result." Tenn. Code Ann. 39-11-106(a)(2). ***An act is premeditated when*** "done after the exercise of reflection and judgment." Tenn. Code Ann. 39-13-202(d). ***Although*** "the intent to kill must have been formed prior to the act itself," ***it need not*** "preexist in the mind of the accused for any definite period of time." *Id.* ***Instead, the accused must be*** "free from excitement and passion as to be capable of premeditation." *Id.* ***A person convicted of first-degree murder may be sentenced to life, life without parole, or death.*** Tenn. Code Ann. 39-13-202(c).

Notice how the statute is broken into portions that the reader needs; the rest is omitted or will be discussed later. Also notice that the non-statutory phrases shown in bold italics connect the statutory phrases. Once again, that's the voice accompanying the reader through the material.

Example 3

Here's an example where the reader is guided through complex provisions involving the internet, interactive computer services, immunity, and content.

> *Congress has deliberately provided broad immunity to interactive computer services for the content its users create. Section 230 provides that* "[n]o provider or user of an interactive computer service shall be treated as the publisher or speaker of any information provided by another information content provider." 47 U.S.C. § 230(c)(*l*). "No cause of action may be brought and no

> liability may be imposed under any State or local law that is inconsistent with this section." *Id.* § 230(e)(3).
>
> *The purpose behind this statutory protection is clear from the statute; Congress explicitly recognized the internet and interactive computer services as proving* "a forum for a true diversity of political discourse, unique opportunities for cultural development, and myriad avenues for intellectual activity." *Id. More importantly, it also found that the internet and interactive computer services* "have flourished, to the benefit of all Americans, with a minimum of government regulation." *Id.* § 230(a)(4) (emphasis added).
>
> *Section 230 provides that* "[n]o provider or user of an interactive computer service shall be treated as the publisher or speaker of any information provided by another information content provider." 47 U.S.C. § 230(c)(*l*). *Absent an exception, service providers are immunized from a state law claim if*: (1) "[they are] a provider or user of an interactive computer service; (2) the claim is based on information provided by another information content provider; and (3) the claim would treat [the provider] as the publisher or speaker of that information."

In short, the reader is given the key portions of the statute with other terms omitted for brevity and readability. The other phrases show the writer's understanding of the material. In contrast, copying and pasting the entirety of section 230 would force the reader to skip the material (at best) or fling your brief across the room (at worst).

D. Case Law Examples

As illustrated earlier, every legal roadmap culminates in "case law examples." You might say they put the "E" in CREAC. That's important because one of the first things we learned in law school was the doctrine of stare decisis, which is a Latin phrase meaning "to stare at the decisis." Okay, that's not true; the loose translation is closer to "been there, done that." In short, courts are supposed to decide similar cases in a similar way.

Identifying when one case is like another requires close reading, critical thinking, and creativity. Remember that a well-written decision includes a statement of the issues, a factual narrative, a discussion of legal principles, an analysis of how the principles apply to the facts, and a holding. If you're thinking, "Hey, those sound like the components of an appellate brief," you're exactly right. Few if any cases are identical. But many have some similarities in the facts, principles, and analysis, that allow you to argue by analogy. Or they have differences that allow you to argue by distinction.

Here's the problem. When discussing case law, appellate briefs often . . . slow . . . to . . . a . . . crawl . . . There are reasons for this. The brief may discuss too many cases. Or the brief addresses the cases in some random order. Or the brief discusses the cases in too much detail.

The key to synthesizing case law is to use the best cases, not the most cases. Be selective. Why are some cases more useful than others?

1. Controlling and Persuasive Authority

We should begin with a quick and basic review of controlling and persuasive authority, so please hand me that broad brush over there. Thanks.

The U.S. Supreme Court's interpretation of federal law must be followed by circuit courts and district courts. A Circuit Court of Appeals' decision must be followed by the district courts in that circuit. A decision by a state's highest court must be followed by all other courts in that state; and a decision by the state's intermediate appellate court must be followed by the lower courts in that state.

That overview can get more nuanced in some cases, but that's the general idea. Thus, in an ideal world, you want your brief filled with controlling authority that is favorable to your case.

If you don't have controlling authority, everything else may be persuasive authority. Therefore, finding a case that is factually and legally the same as your client's case is a good thing regardless of what court wrote the decision. And keep in mind there are degrees in persuasive authority. An appellate decision in another circuit is likely more persuasive than a district court's published decision from that circuit. A decision from another state's supreme court may be more persuasive than one from that state's intermediate appellate court.[1]

2. Summarize Cases with Purpose

When you know what cases to include in the brief, think about how to summarize them as effectively as possible. Of course, it's not enough to simply summarize a bunch of cases; as we will discuss a bit later, effective analysis requires that principles be identified, reconciled, and compared to other cases. But that's a tall order if the brief doesn't tell the reader what the cases are about in the first place.

---

[1] A Tennessee Supreme Court Justice once told me that she found New Jersey Supreme Court opinions particularly persuasive. I didn't ask why. I just nodded along, as though we were either stating the obvious or sharing a secret.

a. Topic Sentence

Imagine a reader who only reads the topic sentence and skims the rest. Which of these provides something of value?

- This is an important case.
- This is an important case about a motorcycle.
- This is an important case about a blue motorcycle that ran off the road and hit a tree.
- This is an important case about a motorcycle with defective brakes.
- In *Miller v. Johnson*, the plaintiff crashed his blue motorcycle into a tree and suffered massive head injuries.
- The New Jersey Supreme Court has said that a manufacturer may be liable for injuries suffered by a plaintiff who bought a motorcycle with defective brakes.

In other words, the topic sentence must give the reader an immediate sense of why they are being told about a specific case. Notice how that is conveyed in these examples.

- A defendant's effort to rob a victim who has just withdrawn cash from an ATM may constitute attempted federal bank robbery. *United States v. McCarter*, 406 F.3d 460 (7th Cir. 2005).
- Threats to kill the victim, procuring a weapon, waiting for a victim's arrival, and firing several shots at close range are probative of premeditation.
- Terminating an employee for reporting the employer's culture of sexual harassment violates Title VII.

- A claim for negligence requires plaintiffs to establish that their injuries were caused by a defendant's actions. *St. Louis v. Benjamin Moore & Co.*, 226 S.W.3d 110, 113 (Mo. 2007).

In contrast, a topic sentence with the name of a case, the full citation, too many facts, or nothing of significance gives the reader nothing to remember. Like these:

- "In *Miller v. Johnson*, the plaintiff, Mike Miller, was injured in a scooter incident in Knoxville, Tennessee on April 1, 2024, and he brought this products liability against Swifty Scooters."
- *People v. Moriarity* is an important decision.
- The aforementioned principles were applied in the case of *State v. McIntyre*.

b. Concise Facts

After the topic sentence, summarize the facts of a case in as few sentences as possible. As we will discuss a bit later, the facts are critical in building or refuting comparisons or analogies. But too many facts can overwhelm the reader. Leave out the procedural history, the proper names of parties and witnesses, and the specific dates or locations.

If you are summarizing a series of criminal cases, just say "the defendant" in each summary, rather than force the reader to distinguish between and keep track of Jim Jones, Bob Johnson, and Jim-Bob Butterbean. In other cases, use terms like "employee," "employer," "victim," and so on. It's a subtle difference, but an important one that allows the reader to compare cases more easily.

c. The Court's Reasoning

As concisely as possible, tell the reader what the court said about the legal principle, factor, or element being discussed and applied. Appellate courts are expected to explain their decisions and show their work. What's more, the court's rationale must make sense when applied to your case. Although you should look for the court's key language to quote, be careful not to go overboard with copying and pasting. (We talked about that earlier.)

d. The Court's Holding

Identifying the court's holding is not always easy. For one thing, courts and lawyers often say "hold" or "held" when they mean something else. A holding is not the court's recitation of the law or other observations. The holding is the court's conclusion when it applies legal principles to the facts of a case. This is easier to understand with examples

- "In *Jones*, the court held that first-degree murder requires premeditation." Nope, that's not a holding. That's just the court pointing out a legal requirement.
- "In *Smith*, the court held that it must consider the totality of the circumstance to decide whether premeditation exists." Nope, that's not a holding either. That's just the court identifying a framework that applies.
- "In *Johnson*, the court held that the evidence was sufficient to establish premeditation because the defendant made threats, obtained a gun, waited in hiding, and shot the victim from close range." Now *that's* a holding.

While we're on the topic, don't mistake dicta for a holding.

- "In *Miller*, the court held that the evidence may have established self-defense if the defendant was in reasonable fear of death or serious bodily injury. But that defense was not raised at trial."

This sounds like a holding, but it's not. This is dicta, which is language that is useful because the court said it, but not all that useful because the court (arguably) didn't *need* to say it. They do that a lot, so beware. Good news. There is an easy fix for this. Don't say hold, held, or holding unless you are certain that what you are about to write is the actual holding in the legal sense of the word. When in doubt, use words like "concluded," "observed," "stated," "noted," "said," and "emphasized."

e. Examples

These suggestions make much more sense with examples, but don't limit yourself to those below. You will read hundreds of opinions and briefs and nearly all of them will try to summarize some key cases. You can evaluate how effective they are. You can identify the components. You can see when they are concise and when they drag on. And you can borrow some ideas from the ones that stand out to you.

Example 1

This summary has a useful topic sentence, two sentences containing the key facts, and the court's rationale.

> An investigator's insertion of a key into the padlock of a storage unit does not constitute an unreasonable search. *United States v. Lyons*, 898 F.2d 210, 211 (1st Cir. 1990). In *Lyons,* FBI agents seized several keys from the defendant after arresting him for drug trafficking charges. *Id.* After learning that a storage unit was rented in the name of the defendant's associate, the agents tested one of the keys in the lock and "relocked the padlock without

> opening the compartment." *Id.* The court reasoned that the agent "merely identified a storage unit to which [the defendant] had access" and that the agent "did not search or seize the contents of the storage unit" before getting a search warrant. *Id.*

Example 2

Here's an excerpt with a solid topic sentence, a few facts, and the court's explanation.

> Attempted bank robbery occurs when a defendant forces a victim to withdraw money from an ATM but flees before taking possession of the money. *United States v. McCarter*, 406 F.3d 460, 463 (7th Cir. 2005). In that case, the victim inserted her ATM card and yelled for help. *Id.* The defendant fled before the victim entered her pin number or withdrew money. *Id.* In affirming the conviction, the court explained that a victim who has been forced to withdraw the money becomes the defendant's "unwilling agent." *Id.* Thus, the money is taken from the care, custody, control or possession of the bank, and not the individual victim." *Id.* at 462.

Example 3

Just for fun, let's see how this same paragraph can get bogged down in stuff that doesn't matter:

> The Seventh Circuit Court of Appeals upheld an attempted bank robbery conviction in *United States v. McCarter*, 406 F.3d 460 (7th Cir. 2005). On April 1, 2002, the defendant, Jim McCarter, approached the victim, Linda Carter, on the corner of Main Street and Tenth Street in Saint Louis, Missouri. McCarter pulled a .38 caliber handgun and told Carter, "Give me your cash." *Id.* When Carter said she did not have any cash, McCarter

> forced her to drive him to the ATM at the First Federal Credit Union. *Id.* McCarter told Carter to insert her card into the ATM and withdraw "at least $300." *Id.* As Carter prepared to do so, a police car pulled up to the ATM, blocked Carter's car, and ordered McCarter out of the car. *Id.* McCarter was arrested and questioned. *Id.* He was later indicted for attempted federal bank robbery. *Id.* McCarter moved to dismiss on the basis that he planned to take money from Carter and not the bank. *Id.* After a hearing on December 1, 2003, the District Court denied the motion by written order. *Id.* The Defendant was convicted by a jury and appealed. The Seventh Circuit reasoned that "money in an ATM is in the 'care, custody, control, management or possession of, any bank." *Id.* at 462-63 (quoting 18 U.S.C. § 2113(a)). Although the money is withdrawn by an individual victim, the court explained that a victim who has been forced to withdraw the money becomes the defendant's "unwilling agent." *Id.* Thus, the money is taken from the care, custody, control or possession of the bank, and not the individual victim." *Id.* at 462. The court affirmed the conviction.

Did you read that one? If so, find a red pen and strike through the passages that made your eyes glaze over.

Example

This case involved a lot of facts and the application of four key factors. But the summary is concise, partly because the factors are identified as they are applied.

> Fourth Amendment protections do not apply to areas outside the curtilage of a home. In *United States v. Dunn*, 480 U.S. 294, 300 (1987), agents made a warrantless entry onto the defendant's property, crossed two fences, and found evidence of drug manufacturing in a barn. *Id.* at

> 297. In evaluating Fourth Amendment protections, the Court concluded that the barn was outside of the protected curtilage of the home. *Id.* at 305. The Court emphasized four factors: the barn was sixty yards from the home, the barn was not contained within the fence that surrounded the home, the barn was not used for activities that were associated with the home, and the defendant made no effort to protect the area from observation. Id. at 301.

In other words, the summary of *Dunn* identified the four-factor analysis while at the same time applying them to the facts. That is another good technique for keeping the relevant content while remaining concise.

f. The Self-Test

These examples have one thing in common: they are the result of trial and error and dozens of revisions. They don't need to be perfect. But they do need to be concise and readable. And they need enough content for the reader to compare them to one another and to your client's case.

As you're writing the brief and summarizing key decisions, always imagine the court is asking you the following questions.

- Why is that case relevant?
- Is that case controlling?
- What happened in that case?
- What was the court's holding in that case?
- How did the court reach that holding?

Likewise, when you're reading the opposing party's brief, ask the same questions. Don't wait for lightning to strike at the oral argument. Know the answers to these questions as you write the brief.

3. Add Substance, Not Length

Not every case needs a full paragraph or a complete page of discourse. Incorporate more with less.

Example 1

In the following example, the topic sentence is written to cover two short case discussions.

> Statements of an unavailable declarant are admissible under Rule 804(b)(1) where the Government's motives for examining a witness before a grand jury were similar to its motives in examining the witness at trial. In *United States v. McFall*, 558 F.3d 951, 963 (9th Cir. 2009), the trial occurred more than two years after the grand jury proceeding and indictment. The court said that Rule 804(b)(1) "does not require an identical quantum of motivation." Likewise, the court in *United States v. Miller*, 904 F.2d 65, 68 (D.C. Cir. 1990) determined that the Government had a "sufficiently similar" motive in examining witnesses before a grand jury or at trial because the testimony was directed at the issue of guilt or innocence.

Example 2

Although you should be wary of long, string citations, citing cases with explanatory parentheticals is an effective way to add more with less.

> Warrantless intrusions into shared spaces do not violate the Fourth Amendment rights of tenants. *See United States v. Sweeney*, 821 F.3d 898, 900 (7th Cir. 2016) (holding that the basement of an apartment did not

> constitute a protected area); *United States v. Villegas*, 495 F.3d 761, 767-68 (7th Cir. 2007) (holding that the Fourth Amendment did not protect the search of an internal duplex hallway); *United States v. Concepcion*, 942 F.2d 1170, 1172 (7th Cir. 1991) (providing that the search of a shared entrance to an apartment building did not violate the Fourth Amendment); *United States v. Boden*, 854 F.2d 983, 990 (7th Cir. 1988) (emphasizing the search of a common area of a rental storage unit facility did not violate the defendant's rights).

Example 3

And this final example covers a lot of ground by combining a number of techniques.

> The United States Supreme Court has exhibited caution when applying principles to digital technology. In *Carpenter v. United States*, 585 U.S. 296, 308 (2018), the Court recognized that it "has been careful not to uncritically extend existing precedents" when "confronting new concerns wrought by digital technology." In that case, the Court invalidated the warrantless seizure and search of cell-phone records revealing the location and movements of a cell-phone user over the course of 127 days. *Id.* at 304. *See Seo v. State*, 148 N.E.3d 952, 961 (Ind. 2020) ("This case underscores several reasons why the narrow exception may be generally unsuitable to the compelled production of any unlocked smartphone."); *Commonwealth v. Davis*, 220 A.3d 534 (Pa. 2019) ("It would be a significant expansion of the foregone conclusion rationale to apply it to a defendant's compelled oral or written testimony.").

And One More Thing

Briefs fail when they have no sense of direction, much less a roadmap. This section gives you several tools that guide courts through the legal principles—the "R" and "E" of a CREAC. As you learn to use them, you will become adept at showing the court how to reach the result you want.

All that's left is to show them why.

CHAPTER X

The Argument: "Reasons"

We have saved the most daunting part of The Argument for last. Why should the court rule in your favor?

In terms of structure, the "why" is the "A" of a CREAC. In terms of affirmation bias, the "why" means overcoming the status quo. In terms of math, the "why" means showing your case is like the 8 percent of cases that merit relief and not like the 92 percent of cases that don't. In terms of prevailing for your client, the *"why"* means pretty much everything.

A. Transition to the Application

As you begin to apply the legal principles and examples to the facts of your case for any given issue, you may be tempted to meet the moment with something formal and elaborate. But all you really need is one word.

Here.

That's the word, in all its modesty. It tells the reader to wake up, things are about to get real. Enough reading "the law," it's time to start talking about *this* case, *this dispute*.

- Here, the Government's conduct was blatant and unconscionable.
- Here, the Defendant committed malpractice.
- Here, the Defendant breached the contract.
- Here, there simply was no infringement.
- Here, the Plaintiff assumed the risk.

If you want to personalize things or simply add some variety, use the *name of your client* or the opposing party.

- Anna Fender was denied due process.
- Dr. Wyatt Riot was entitled to summary judgment.
- Electrocuting Fred Gundy would be cruel and unusual.
- A-Mark breached the contract.
- Grumhold submitted false data.
- Wally Squally acted with premeditation.

Here, nothing elaborate is needed.

B. Make Your Strongest Points

Begin with your strongest points. Don't worry (for now) about the opposing arguments or the lower court's reasoning.

1. Apply the Facts

Apply the legal principles to the facts. If readers have followed your roadmap through the rules and examples, they are ready to hear about your case. With that in mind, the facts don't just tell the story; they are the critical part of the analysis. You need not recite the entire statement of facts in the "A" of CREAC, but you should emphasize the facts that bear upon an element or factor. Go back and review your statement of facts; the legally relevant facts are often those that appear in both the statement of the facts and the argument. For that matter, a judge may skim through the statement of facts to get into the argument. So, apply the facts thoroughly.

Example 1

Let's say a roadmap of legal principles included the four-part test for determining whether a search occurred on property near a home. *United States v. Dunn*, 480 U.S. 294, 301 (1987), Notice how this passage concisely applies the facts to each of the four parts.

> Here, the designated camping space on which Mr. Grimes' home was erected was curtilage under the four factors in *Dunn*. First, it was in "proximity" and directly adjacent to Mr. Grimes' home. Second, marked boundaries of the campsite visibly designated and enclosed Mr. Grimes' assigned camping area. Third, Mr. Grimes used the area as an extension of his home. Mr. Grimes' 12x9 tent was surrounded by a covered vestibule, which he called a "porch." Finally, Mr. Grimes used this area for private activities.

That entire paragraph consists of facts about the client's case; they are the key. By the way, if you want to take your analysis to the next level, insert photographs or other material from the record to bolster your arguments. Show *and* tell.

Example 2

Applying the facts presents an opportunity to highlight or even quote material from the record, exhibits or testimony. Remember the Boston bombing case that we talked about earlier? One of the issues in that case involved jury selection and media exposure. After summarizing the legal framework, the Government's brief argued that the trial court did not abuse its discretion because it took elaborate steps to pick the jury. Doing that meant focusing on the facts in the record. (In this excerpt, the argument is also citing the record on appeal and the appendix.)

> The district court began by summoning an "expanded jury pool," with 1373 citizens reporting for jury selection. Pet. App. 223a n.2; *see id.* at 27a. The court directed each of them to complete under oath "a long and detailed one-hundred-question questionnaire" that had been "jointly developed" with the parties. *Id.* at 223a n.2, 249a; *see id.* at 350a-383a. The questionnaire required prospective jurors to list their "primary source[s] of news," with specific follow-ups about print, television, radio, and internet sources. Id. at 371a. It then asked how prospective jurors would "describe the amount of media coverage [they] have seen about this case," whether a "lot," a "moderate" amount, a "little," or "[n]one." *Id.* at 372a. And Question 77 asked each prospective juror (1) whether "[a]s a result of what [he or she] ha[d] seen or read in the news media," he or she had "formed an opinion" that respondent was "guilty" or "not guilty," or "should" or "should not" "receive the death penalty," and (2) if so, whether he or she would be "able or unable to set aside [that] opinion and base [his or her] decision about guilt and punishment solely on the evidence that will be presented * * * in court." *Id.* at 373a.
>
> The questionnaire enabled the district court, in consultation with the parties, to conduct an initial screen of the first half of the jury pool and excuse nearly two thirds (441 of 697) of those prospective jurors. *See* Pet.

> App. 30a; C.A. App. 3866, 3894. That process provided a narrower, but still substantial, pool of 256 prospective jurors for individual *voir dire* for fitness to serve on the 12-person jury. Pet. App. 30a. 'The court and the parties then engaged in a "time-consuming" and tailored "face-to-face, give-and-take" [discussions]. The district court also allowed the parties what respondent's counsel at the time called "considerable latitude" to ask follow-up questions—including on pretrial publicity. CA. App. 1143; see, e.g., J.A. 317-318, 331-332, 350, 371-372, 407-412, 455-456 (defense follow-up on pretrial publicity during voir dire of seated jurors). Based on the individualized questioning, the district court excused numerous prospective jurors for cause. See Pet. App. 35a. And each side was able to exercise 23 peremptory strikes. *See id.* at 224a, 235.

The brief goes on in that fashion for several more pages describing the details in that case. Nothing but facts. The Government's brief later compared the case to other cases and addressed the opposing arguments. But its focus in the A of the CREAC was initially on the facts that showed the trial court exercised its discretion properly.

Example 3

After setting out the legal principles regarding the Eighth Amendment, the analysis turns to the "A" of the CREAC and uses factual details to paint a bleak picture:

> Mr. Munson's punishment is cruel and unusual. As the trial court noted, he has lived in solitary confinement for 35 years. For twenty-three and one-half hours of each day, he is isolated in a cell "roughly the size of a standard parking space." There is no window. The bed has a thin mattress and a threadbare blanket. There is a "stainless-

> steel toilet and sink." The cell walls are solid white, and the floor is made of "pure concrete." There is no carpet.

Like the earlier example, this would be a good time to include a picture from the record to bolster your description.

Example 4

Here, the legal principles discussed the right of publicity and the defense of transformation. Once again, when the analysis turned to the "A" of the CREAC, the initial focus was on the facts.

> The Plaintiff's claim was properly rejected because the default avatar in the Defendant's Spaceball is not a literal depiction. First, the default avatar's appearance differed from Plaintiff's. Second, the default avatar's performance metrics differed from Plaintiff's in nearly every statistical category. Third, the default avatar's jersey does not bear Plaintiff's name or his team's name. Rather, the game user can input any writing they choose.

2. *Apply Favorable Precedent*

Stare decisis means that courts decide similar cases in a similar way. Usually. So, after carefully applying the legal principles to the facts, compare the facts to other cases. No two cases are exactly alike, but your task is to show that your case is similar or analogous. The law is whatever it is. But if the facts are similar, then the result should be the same, right? And if the court's rationale underlying its decision in a prior case is served when applied to your case, the result should be the same, right?

That's the idea, anyway. Here are a few ways to bring that idea to the page.

a. Compare as You Go

As you apply the legal principles to the facts of your case, comparisons with other cases should become apparent. As they do, drop them into the analysis. Notice how this is accomplished below (and shown in italics).

Example

> However inflammatory, the material B.P. posted on his social media was not substantially connected to the school. *Like the student in Mahoney*, B.P. made the posts on his own phone, on his own time, and on his own social media account. Although his posts referred to the name of his school, his football coach, and a group of unidentified students, they were addressed to his own ten or twelve followers and friends. *As in Johnson*, the circulation of a single digital screen shot, by itself, does not amount to a substantial connection.
>
> And even if those facts were enough to connect the posts to the school, they did not result in a material disruption. *In Tinker, for example, the Court emphasized that the students' draft protest did not interrupt classroom instruction. Likewise, this case lacks evidence of classroom instruction.* At most, the school principal cut a pep rally short by about five minutes after learning about the social media posts. That is not a material disruption.

b. Bolster the Authority

In addition to the comparisons, remind the reader of the controlling weight of the authority. Here's a modified version of the above passage.

Here, the facts resemble Mahoney, which the Court decided just last year. Like the student in *Mahoney*, B.P. posted material on social media that was not substantially connected to the school. He made the posts on his own phone, on his own time, and on his own social media account. Although his posts referred to the name of his school, his football coach, and a group of unidentified students, they were addressed to his own ten or twelve followers and friends. Although a single digital screen shot was taken and, predictably, circulated at school, no one at the school was mentioned by name.

And even if that were enough to connect the posts to the school, they did not result in a material disruption as explained in *Tinker—a case that has protected the freedom of expression for over fifty years*. The school principal simply cut a pep rally short by about five minutes after learning about the social media posts. *In short, the trial court applied basic legal principles that have been well-established for decades and reaffirmed less than a year ago*. This court should follow suit.

Here are a few more suggestions for bolstering comparisons to other cases. Mix and match for all sorts of fun.

- Nearly every court that has addressed this issue has reached the same conclusion.
- The Court of Appeals applied controlling case law; indeed, the most recent decision is just a little over a year old.
- The trial court chose the approach followed by an overwhelming majority of courts.
- Without exception, courts have held that schools may regulate a student's "vulgar speech."

- Ms. Doe's case is controlled by *Stevens,* which this court decided just last year.
- Like the student in *Stevens,* Ms. Doe's right to freedom of expression was disregarded.
- Much like the university held liable just last year in *Stevens*, the Defendant refused to investigate.
- Here, the Defendant engaged in precisely the same conduct that has been condemned by every court that has addressed the issue.

In short, you're not just comparing your case to a prior case; you're comparing your case to strong, well-established, long-standing case law.

c. Detailed Reminders

When making comparisons, be sure to add the legally relevant details about the prior case. No one expects (or wants) you to completely re-summarize a case that was discussed earlier. But a refresher is useful when several pages separate a case that was discussed as an example in the "E" of a CREAC and a comparison that is later made in the "A" of the CREAC.

In the following examples, notice how the readers' memories are refreshed to make the comparisons crystal clear.

Example 1

> *Like the students who wore the armbands to protest the draft* in *Tinker*, Mr. Thomas experienced minimal responses to his shirt from other students at Plymouth Rock High School. For example, *like the football player who warned the protesting student*s in *Tinker*, a couple of students hassled Mr. Thomas during lunch. Even though someone pushed Mr. Thomas, causing his lunch tray to fall to the floor, the whole incident lasted only a few minutes.

In Tinker, the Court emphasized that nothing that occurred resulted in any discipline or punishment. Likewise, not a single student was disciplined for the conduct involving Mr. Thomas. Indeed, Mr. Thomas reacted to the lunchroom incident by simply ignoring the hecklers. But even if the lunchroom incident qualifies as some form of actual disruption, it was no more disruptive than what happened in *Tinker*. The Court in *Tinker* recognized that a student's free speech "does not end at the school door." So, too, should this court.

Example 2

Not only does *Burton* reflect the majority rule, the facts are also almost identical to our case. *In Burton, the victim withdrew $150 from an ATM and handed it to the defendant. The Fifth Circuit vacated the defendant's conviction for bank robbery because the defendant stole money from the victim after the victim withdrew money from the ATM*. Likewise, Mr. Murphy stole money from Ms. James, not from her bank. He stalked Ms. James as she pulled up to an ATM and made a withdrawal; he then accosted Ms. James. The victim reached into her purse and handed Murphy a roll of twenty-dollar bills. At that point, the money had been withdrawn by the victim and was entirely in her possession. There is no dispute that Mr. Murphy took the money from Ms. James's hand and fled. But just as in *Burton*, this conduct was not federal bank robbery.

Example 3

No court has invalidated solitary confinement in cases like this one. Like *the inmate in Miller, who served 23 hours each day in solitary confinement*, the plaintiff is not in complete isolation. He is allowed to be outside of his cell for one hour each day, and he has a limited number of phone calls per month. *As discussed above, an inmate's claim was rejected in Johnson where he had contact with medical personnel and a religious leader at least once a month.* Here, the plaintiff had unlimited access to medical care and chose not to avail himself of religious consultation.

d. Add Substance, Not Length

The Bluebook allows us to use explanatory parentheticals after citing authority.[1] They don't replace analysis, but they sure can bolster it. In this example, the cases show that the same principle has been applied in a variety of scenarios.

Here, the Defendant may have had a right to counsel post-indictment, but he did not have a right to counsel pre-indictment. In *Maine v. Moulton*, 474 U.S. 159 (1985), the Court held that where surreptitious government surveillance produced evidence of two crimes, the defendant's right to counsel attached only to the crime for which defendant had been indicted. *See also United States v. Gouveia*, 467 U.S. 180 (1984) (citing *Kirby*, Supreme Court overturned the Ninth Circuit holding that administrative detention serves an accusatory function necessitating the right to counsel to ensure a fair trial).

Likewise, the Defendant received a letter saying that he was the subject of a grand jury matter, and he was the subject of a search warrant that was executed at his residence. But he had not been formally charged. As in *United States v. Moody*, 206 F.3d 609, 612 (6th 2000), the right to counsel simply did not attach where government had not "initiat[ed] judicial criminal proceedings . . . by

[1] *The Bluebook, A Uniform System of Citation*, B10.1.5.

> way of formal charge[s]." *See also Moran v. Burbine*, 475 U.S. 412, 430 (1986) (holding that "the possibility that [certain government actions] may have important consequences at trial, standing alone, is insufficient to trigger the Sixth Amendment right to counsel"). Thus, the trial court correctly denied the Defendant's motion to suppress.

Simple, yet effective. Explanatory parentheticals also may be employed when using a string cite to show a range of examples from several jurisdictions. Judges may not want to read all those cases; but they may appreciate a quick glimpse. (Their law clerks sure will.) And they may even be impressed with the extent of your research. That has to help at least a little, right?

C. Address Opposing Arguments

After you apply the legal principles to the facts of your case and compare those facts to favorable cases under the banner of stare decisis, what else is left for the analysis to do? If you're the appellant, remember that the lower court did something wrong, and the opposing party is defending that ruling. If you're the appellee, you know that the appellant is trying to upset the status quo.

In short, you must address opposing arguments. Seems pretty obvious, huh? But I can't tell you how often that is overlooked or simply left to the court to figure out on its own.

1. Dealing with Facts

We started the application by applying the legal principles to the facts of the case. But also think about the absence of facts, as shown in this example.

> While claiming that the evidence of premeditation was sufficient, the prosecution points to none of the

> evidence often emphasized in prior cases. There was no evidence, for example, that the defendant was lying-in-waiting. No evidence that he took steps to procure a weapon in advance. No evidence that he threatened to kill the victim. No evidence of multiple gunshots. Nothing of the sort. All that's left is evidence that the defendant argued with the victim and fired a single shot that struck the victim in the hip. Although tragic, the outcome was not the product of a premeditated intent to kill.

In short, when refuting the other side's arguments, feel free to point out what the evidence did *not* show.

2. Distinguishing Precedent

The most common way of handling cases relied on by the lower court or opposing party is to point out they involve different facts or issues. Arguing by distinction can be just as effective as arguing by analogy. The cases aren't wrong, the argument goes, they are simply different. In fact, it's even possible that they are both right. Two things can be true, as they say.

Example 1

This is the above paragraph with references to distinguishable cases. As for as we know, the cases are all decidedly correctly. It just happens they are different.

> While claiming that the evidence of premeditation was sufficient, the prosecution points to none of the evidence often emphasized in prior cases. There was no evidence, for example, that the defendant was lying-in-waiting, as in *Miller*. No evidence that he took steps to procure a weapon in advance, as in *Stevens, Davis, Powers*, and numerous other cases. No evidence that he threatened to kill the victim, as in *Miller* and *Norman*. No

evidence of multiple gunshots, cited in numerous cases in which courts properly upheld the sufficiency of the evidence. But here, there is nothing of the sort. Nothing of the sort. All that's left is evidence that the defendant argued with the victim and fired a single shot that struck the victim in the hip. Although tragic, the outcome was not the product of a premeditated intent to kill.

Example 2

Defendant's actions are distinguishable from those of the defendant in *Charles*. In *Charles*, the court found that allegations of criminal actions on the part of an HOA developer were within the scope of community well-being because HOAs hold quasi-governmental powers and affect communities in ways like governmental entities. Here, Defendant had no connections with Mr. Miller's HOA. Whereas the defendant in *Charles* made statements concerning the malfeasance of the HOA developer, the Defendant's video had no bearing on any issue related to the HOA. In short, the present case does not fit within the "community well-being" as defined in *Charles*.

Example 3

In *Chen*, the Court understandably found that a student's racially charged and profane speech caused a substantial disruption. Students protested what they perceived to be administrators' inaction. ~~Students were bullied and harassed.~~ Police were called to the school to quell a number of disturbances. Class time was used to discuss the incidents and the harm they inflicted. Numerous students missed school; some even transferred. Not surprisingly, the court agreed there had been a material and substantial disruption.

In stark contrast, the "substantial disruption" in this case amounted to a brief, five-minute disruption at a pep rally and discussions during a class period that were outside of the lesson plans. As the trial court correctly recognized, that's a far cry from what happened in *Chen*.

Example 4

The Government's argument that testing a key in a lock is not a search hinges on *United States v. Lyons*, 898 F.2d 210 (1st Cir. 1990). That case is entirely different from Mr. Magnum's. In *Lyons*, the storage unit was rented by an associate of Lyons, not Lyons himself. In contrast, Mr. Magnum had exclusive access to his own storage unit.

Example 5

Although the Government has also relied on *United States v. DeBardeleben*, 740 F.2d 440 (6th Cir. 1984), that case involved a key to a car and not a key to a storage unit. What's more, the defendant in that case altered the license plate so that officers were unable to identify its owner. In short, *DeBardeleben* simply does not apply.

3. *Misrepresenting Precedent*

For even more fun, point out that the opposing side has misread (or even misrepresented) authority. Here are some examples and templates that work well.

Example 1

The Government claims that *DiNapoli* "held that parties do not have the same level of intensity when questioning witnesses in the grand jury and, therefore, do not have similar motive." But that language doesn't appear in the opinion. Moreover, the court in *DiNapoli* analyzed the intensity of questioning as one factor to be considered. When properly understood, *DiNapoli* supports Mr. Magnum's position, not the Government's.

Example 2

Although Defendant cites *Miller* for the principle that good faith is a complete defense, that case says nothing of the sort. What the court *does* say is blah blah blah. And what the court *does* hold is yadda, yadda, yadda.

Example 3

The defendant cites Case A for the holding that such and such. That is not the holding of Case A. At best, the language cited by the defendant is dicta. And even if that is the holding, that doesn't help the defendant because the case is distinguishable.

Example 4

The Government's reliance on *Michigan v. Bryant* is misplaced because that case was limited to the relationship between interrogation, hearsay, and the Confrontation Clause. In contrast, there was no interrogation in this case. Second, the *Bryant* case involved an ongoing emergency. Here, Dr. Campbell's report followed an investigation that had deliberately targeted Stephenson with the goal of creating evidence that could positively identify him as the murderer at trial. Third, the fact that Dr. Campbell conducted her analysis in her own facility does not mean that the report was non-testimonial in nature. Indeed, the Government approached Dr. Campbell, provided her with evidence, and tasked her with comparing an image of a shooter at the scene of a crime and another image of a man they suspected to be involved. In short, nothing in *Bryant* sanctions the Government's conduct in this case.

4. Diminishing Precedent

Remember how you can bolster favorable authority? You may be able to do the opposite. Here are some ideas to get you going; once you get the idea, you'll see more examples in nearly every opinion or brief you read.

- The Plaintiff relies on an unpublished decision in *Miller v. Hampton.*
- The Defendant relies on a single decision.
- The Defendant relies on *Singletary*, which was decided long before the popular use of digital technology.
- The Defendant admits that *Jackson* reflects a minority view.
- The Defendant relies on a decision that has never been relied on by another court; in fact, it has not even been *cited* by another court in over twenty years.
- The principle has been frequently criticized.

And, if all else fails, argue that the case should be overruled because it was wrongly decided, is no longer workable, or reflects a minority view. Those are valid reasons for courts to depart from stare decisis, though it may be an uphill battle. Of course, remember that a court of appeals cannot overrule or depart from stare decisis when it comes to controlling authority.

D. Statutory Arguments

1. *Reading Statutes*

Reading statutes is like reading Shakespeare: they must be read slowly, and close attention must be paid to terms like "if," "and," "or," "wherefore," "art thou," and "et tu." Given their complexity, statutes can be hard to interpret and summarize. The good news is everyone follows much the same approach.

> Step one. Break the statute into smaller parts (elements) This may be a concise statute with two elements; for example, a first-degree murder statute that requires intent and premeditation. Or it may be a more complex statute—tax, bankruptcy, health law, etc.—that has dozens of elements.
>
> Step two. Define each element. If you're lucky, a statutory element is defined in that same statute or some other statute. For example, the first-degree murder statute may contain a definition of premeditation. So, you need to look no farther. But here's the thing. When a statutory definition itself has elements, you often need to go back to step one.
>
> Step three. If an element is not defined by statute, a court likely has defined it in a prior opinion. So, go find that case.
>
> Step four. Repeat the process.

2. *Interpreting Statutes*

a. Plain Meaning

If the statute or a statutory element is unambiguous, the court simply applies its plain meaning. Courts often find a plain meaning in Black's Law Dictionary or some other dictionary. Sometimes they cite numerous dictionaries. You can, too.

b. Legislative Intent and History

If the statute is ambiguous (susceptible to more than one meaning), the court must apply or define the statute in a way that furthers the legislative intent or purpose. If you're lucky, that purpose may be stated in the statute. If you're slightly less lucky, the purpose may be found in legislative history.

Finding legislative history means reviewing the statements made by a bill's sponsor, other legislative statements, committee notes, and even prior versions of the statute. In past years, this meant combing through archived documents or even listening to legislative discussions found on cassette tapes. Fortunately, that's much easier when researching legislative history in the digital age. In any event, examining why the legislation was proposed and reviewing earlier drafts of a proposed statute offers insight into the legislative intent in enacting the final version of a statute.

And yes, that is all nearly as much fun as it sounds.

c. Canons of Construction

In some cases, courts go beyond the statutory language and legislative history and look to other interpretative principles. Some of these so-called canons have cool Latin names like "ejusdem generis," which means, "Flip a coin," and "expressio unius est exclusio alterius," which means, "How about the best two out of three?"

Just kidding. There are dozens of canons of construction; in fact, there's probably a canon that will support whatever you need the statute to mean. Here are just a few examples.

i. Esjudem Generis

This canon means "of the same kind." When a statute contains a list of specific terms, other items may be encompassed by that statute only if they are like the specified terms. In other words, you should use the items in the statute to determine which objects and things the legislature meant to include.

For example, if a statute refers to someone who operates "planes, trains, and automobiles," a court might use the esjudem generis canon to find that the statute includes someone who operates a motorized scooter because a motorized scooter has a motor. But it does not include someone who rides a bicycle.

Get it?

ii. Expressio Unius Est Exclusio Alterius

This canon means that "the expression of one thing is the exclusion of another. If things are included or specified in the law, an intention to exclude all other things may be inferred. If, for instance, a statute mentions losses caused by "fires," then it does not cover losses for damages caused by "wind." You often see this principle expressed like this: "The statute says X. Had the legislature intended for the statute to also include Y, the statute would simply say so." In other words, pay attention to what the statute does *not* say.

iii. The Entire Act

The statutory text must be examined as a whole and not in isolation. For example, elements should be given the same meaning throughout an entire statutory act. This falls under the heading of common sense or a canon of construction I like to call "duh." Why should a term used multiple times in the same statutory act be given two different meanings?

iv. State of the Law

The legislature is presumed to know the state of the law when it enacts new legislation. These days that may be giving most legislative bodies way too much credit. But at least in theory, they do not intend to change or alter existing law without saying so. As a result, the interpretation of a statute should be reconciled with other statutes and case law.

v. Constitutionality

Statutory provisions are presumed to be constitutional. They may not be. But we start with that premise.

3. *Example*

I know what you're thinking. "Hey Barckhoff, these canons of construction are super-interesting, but could you wrap this up with some sort of practical example?" Glad you asked.

Let's look at a case in which the defendant was convicted of aggravated assault after stabbing the victim in the neck with a tire iron.[2] He was sentenced to 60 days in jail,[3] which seems kind of light when you consider that he STABBED SOMEONE IN THE NECK WITH A TIRE IRON. But he was also placed on probation for several years.[4] As a condition of probation, he was ordered to reimburse the victim's insurance carrier for expenses incurred in paying the victim's medical benefits.[5]

So far, so good. But the applicable statute said only that a court could require a defendant to pay restitution to the "victim of the offense." The key element of that statute, obviously, is the word "victim," but the statute did not define the term. Nor did any

---

2 *State v. Alford*, 970 S.W.2d 944, 945 (Tenn. 1998).

3 *Id.*

4 *Id.*

5 *Id.*

other statute.[6] No one would doubt that the guy with THE TIRE IRON STICKING OUT OF HIS NECK was a victim, but the statute said nothing about insurance carriers.

Given that the term was arguably ambiguous, the defendant (and the court) had to look elsewhere. The legislative history was silent on the matter, which meant either the legislators didn't intend to include insurance companies or (more likely) that the idea simply never occurred to them. Either way, that didn't help. Neither did canons like esjudem generis.

In reviewing the entirety of the criminal sentencing act, however, the defendant noted that other statutes referred to victims' "relatives" and "next of kin" in cases where the victim was deceased.

"Ah-ha," someone may have said.

An insurance company can't be deceased. (In fact, it seems like they never die, but I digress.) They don't have "relatives," and they sure don't have "kin." (Although one could say a company has a parent company but set that aside.) That may be significant. In addition, the legislature is presumed to know the state of the law, so they know an insurance company's payment of medical expenses is a contractual obligation and not something ordinarily prompted by a criminal sentencing scheme.

And if all that weren't enough, the defendant emphasized that if the legislature had intended to include insurance companies as victims who were entitled to restitution—all together now—*it would have simply said so*.

So, there you go. The guy who was stabbed in the neck was a victim entitled to restitution. Seems only right.

---

[6] Tenn. Code Ann. § 40-35-304(a).

E. Comfort Arguments

Courts are required to apply legal principles and resolve disputes. Whereas advocates are tasked with making their best *arguments*, courts have to determine the correct *answer*. That is not easy. And regardless of what they decide, only half of the parties will agree with them. With that in mind, be creative. Think about what courts like to do and what they do not like to do. Think about ways to make their job more comfortable (if not easier).

1. Case Law

We know that courts try to resolve similar cases in the same way. That's the entire point of stare decisis. So, build your points in that way.

- Note that your argument is supported by controlling authorities.
- And then bolster that point by noting the controlling authority has been settled law for X number of years.
- And then bolster *that* point by showing that the controlling authority is consistent with decisions in other jurisdictions.
- And then support *that* point by noting that the controlling authority is fair, efficient, workable, and consistent with the administration of justice.

Here are more examples of putting the court's mind at ease:

- The trial court applied well-established principles and reached a predictable and equitable result.
- For generations, courts have followed *Tinker*'s admonition that first amendment rights do not end at the schoolhouse gate. So, too, should this court.

- This court should simply follow the bright line approach adopted in *Miller* less than a year ago.
- The trial court exercised its discretion in accordance with principles expressed by this court on numerous occasions.

Ready for some real amusement? Flip the script and point out things for the court, as an institution, to worry about. Argue (in good faith of course) that the opposing party's argument would implicitly overrule a line of case. That the trial court's decision overlooked controlling principles. That the opposing argument would create a slippery slope of some sort: increased litigation, a wrong with no remedy, unfairness, and so on. Point out when the opposing party or a lower court relies on case law that has not been cited (much less followed) by later courts.

Here are a few more ideas to get you going:

- However well-intended its result, the trial court missed the critical point of the Supreme Court's decision in *Tinker*.
- No court has ever extended the *Bryson* principle that far.
- At bottom, the Government asks this Court to allow the Government to approach an expert witness, provide her with images that were unlawfully obtained, and then task her with creating an image of a "perpetrator" for use at trial. Not surprisingly, not a single decision has gone this far.
- Anything other than a reversal will signal that the Court has retreated from its holdings in *Johnson* and *Miller*.

- The appellant invites the court to create an unnecessary and counterproductive per se rule that denies administrators the discretion to apply standards on a local, case by case basis. Not surprisingly, the appellant cites no authority for this novel rule.
- If the lower court's judgment is upheld, officers will not know how to legally collect evidence, and prosecutors will no longer trust that evidence is admissible at trial.

2. *Statutes*

Comfort arguments work here, too. As we discussed earlier, courts look at the plain language of a statute; if the language is unambiguous, that ends the matter. But if the statutory language is ambiguous, the court will look to things like legislative history and cannons of construction.

None of that is a secret. That's the playbook everyone follows when examining statutes. Create your arguments accordingly.

- The trial court correctly applied the plain meaning of the statute.
- Because the trial court correctly determined that the statutory language is unambiguous, there is no need to resort to legislative history.
- This court need only apply what is plain on the face of the statute and nothing more.
- Even if the defendant is correct that the statutory language is ambiguous, the trial court's ruling is supported by ample legislative history.

- Because the statute is arguably ambiguous, the Court of Appeals correctly resorted to the statutory scheme as a whole. is supported by the overall statutory scheme.
- As the Court of Appeals observed, the legislature is intended to know the state of the law when it enacts legislation.
- The trial court correctly noted there is no reason to think the legislature would have wanted the same word to have two different meanings.

And now flip the script.

- Because the statute is unambiguous, this court should decline the plaintiff's invitation to view legislative history.
- The Plaintiff's argument defies the plain language of the statute.
- The Plaintiff's argument might be stronger if the statute said "ABC." But it does not.
- The trial court's interpretation of section 101 undermines legislative intent as reflected in ample legislative history.
- By expanding the scope of the statute, the trial court simply disregarded the well-known principle of *esjudem generis*.
- Nothing in the statute supports the Defendant's claim. Indeed, had Congress intended for the statute to apply in consumer protection actions, it would have simply said so.

And everyone's favorite:

- This court should not rewrite the statute.

And One More Thing

Despite your best efforts, the court may disagree. That's why judges get to wear the robes and sit a few feet above you. But if you use and build upon the ideas in this chapter, you will apply the legal principles and examples to the facts, argue by analogy and distinction, address opposing arguments, make the court comfortable, and so on. In short, you will have done everything you can do. That's really all anyone can ask.

PART FOUR

Revisions

CHAPTER XI

Making Revisions: Organization

If you think of legal writing as legal thinking, then it follows that readers should be able to follow your analysis every step of the way. Let's look at ways to make sure they can.

A. Headings and Subheadings

1. Arguments

As we talked about, point headings reveal the conclusions the court should reach and provide structure for your arguments. To make them stand out on the page, they are found in headings and subheadings. Remember these examples?

I. The Defendants violated the Plaintiff's First Amendment right to freedom of speech.

   A. Plaintiff's son's speech was limited to the followers on his private social media page and was not connected to his high school.

B. Plaintiff's son's speech did not cause any material or foreseeable disruption to his high school.

Any readers who glance at those headings know what the case is about. They learn that the main topic has been broken into smaller parts. And they see how the points follow from and support the other.

Here's another example:

I. Plaintiff was entitled to first amendment protection.

A. In *Garcetti*, the Supreme Court held that a public employee's speech outside the scope of their employment is protected under the first amendment.

B Plaintiff's speech was protected by the first amendment because it was outside the scope of her employment as a tenured professor at a public university.

C Plaintiff's speech was entitled to first amendment protection under academic freedom principles.

In addition to serving as roadmaps, headings and subheadings also provide rest stops. Have you ever read a book and looked ahead to see how many pages were left in a chapter so that you could take a break? The same is true here.

2. Facts

Headings and subheadings are also useful in the Statement of the Case or the Statement of Facts. For one thing, they can break an extensive narrative into smaller parts. Take this age-old cautionary tale, for example, and imagine these subheadings are in the Statement of the Facts:

Defendant Meets Victim

Defendant and Victim Get Together

Victim Ends Relationship

Defendant Stalks Victim

Victim Gets Order of Protection

Defendant Violates Order of Protection

Victim Disappears

Officers Investigate

Defendant Gives Statement

Victim's Body Found

Defendant Indicted for First Degree Murder

That may be overkill (pun unintended), but you get the idea. Think of those headings as chapters in a book. Or this example, in a case with extensive pretrial proceedings on key issues:

Procedural History

Pretrial Hearing: Expert Testimony

Pretrial Hearing: Suppression Issue.

Trial Proceedings

Judgment

Post-Trial Hearings

B. Paragraphs

Another key for turning legal writing into legal thinking is paragraph structure. The good news is there's not much new to say about paragraphs. Or if there is, I didn't hear about it. You've been writing and reading them nearly your entire life. But here are some reminders.

1. Length

A well-constructed paragraph can be anywhere from one sentence to several sentences to several pages. But long paragraphs are taxing on a tired reader. Shorter paragraphs allow the reader to track your key points and, well, they just look better on the page.

See?

On the other hand, a long paragraph may be the ticket when you want the reader to gloss over something (like some unfavorable facts). The lesson? As always, be aware of what you're doing and how it affects the reader.

2. Structure

Regardless of its length, a paragraph must be well-structured. We learned in middle school to write a topic sentence and then make sure the supporting sentences in that paragraph relate to that topic. When the topic changes, start a new paragraph (or else risk a paragraph that's too long or some other potential punishment).

A topic sentence should be written as though it may be the only thing a busy reader digests.

Let me repeat that.

A topic sentence should be written as though it may be the only thing a busy reader digests. It needs to be concise, but it also needs to be useful. Look back at the many examples in this guide and look at them from this perspective. In addition, here are some "before and after" examples.

Example 1

- The video recording was harmful.
- By labeling Mr. Magoo as an "idiot" and "epic failure," the published recording had disastrous effects on his reputation, financial well-being, and personal life.

Example 2

- Workout Pros is an exercise app.
- Workout Pros is an app that generates physical workout and diet recommendations for millions of users.

Example 3

- In *Miller*, the defendant raised a good faith defense.
- Although A-Mark corporation cites *Miller* for the principle that good faith is a complete defense, that case says nothing of the sort.

Example 4

- The defendant resided at 15115 Main Street.
- Here, officers staked out the defendant's home at 15115 Main Street and obtained recordings for over two weeks.

Example 5

- Courts have addressed this issue many times.
- Courts agree that long-term, continuous video surveillance is a severe intrusion into an individual's privacy.

Notice that the alternative provides more information for the reader. Of course, we always hope the reader continues reading the entire paragraph. But if they don't, they can't say they didn't get something of use. Yes, I just dropped a triple negative on you. (That reminds me, the next chapter will talk about sentence clarity.)

C. Transitions

You know what? On second thought, we should do more than *hope* readers read the entire paragraph; we should make it easy for them to do so. Every sentence should relate to the others within a paragraph. And every paragraph should relate to the previous paragraph.

Transitions make these relations possible. They can be used to introduce, enumerate, compare contrast, and conclude.

1. Traditional Transitions

- Enumerate:
    - First, second, third, finally
- Compare:
    - Similarly, likewise, in addition, additionally, moreover, furthermore
- Contrast:
    - In contrast, however, conversely
- Conclude:
    - In conclusion, accordingly, thus, therefore

2. Alternative Transitions

- Enumerate:
    - To begin with, also, yet another, still more, what's more

- Similarity:
    - Once again, that is true even when, in a similar vein, as well, as here, much like this case, so too here
- Contrast:
    - But, not so, nor, yet, instead, differs from, on the other hand
- Conclude:
    - As a result, at bottom, in short, in sum, in essence, after all, for that reason, and so, to that end.

3. *Style*

A variety of transitions add a conversational tone and clarity to your writing. They can even create momentum or a sense of urgency. Compare the following examples.

Example 1

First, notice that this topic sentence introduces the topic but does little else. The supporting sentences in the paragraph are connected with mostly traditional transitions (placed in bold as examples). As we'll discuss more in the next chapter, the sentences are also weighed down with some extra words and phrases.

> This Court must apply the **aforementioned landmark case** of *Tinker* to the **facts and circumstances of the case at bar**. In *Tinker*, the students were punished for wearing armbands to protest the draft. **Similarly, in the case at bar**, the plaintiff was punished for wearing a tee-shirt that supported the legalization of marijuana. **However**, the evidence in the record is **devoid of proof** establishing that the plaintiff caused a material or

> substantial disruption. In addition, the defendant may argue that the plaintiff caused a material disruption because several students yelled at him, and one student knocked his tray to the ground. **However,** that argument is unavailing **because of the fact that** the incident lasted a short period of time, and no one was punished. **Accordingly,** this Court should **reach the conclusion** that the **grant of summary judgment to the defendant by the trial court was erroneous.**

Now let's try that with a better topic sentence and some alternative, lighter transitions.

> **Like the students** who wore the armbands to protest the draft in *Tinker*, Mr. Thomas experienced some minimal responses to his shirt from other students at Plymouth Rock High School. **For example**, like the football player who warned the protesting students in *Tinker*, a couple of jocks hassled Mr. Thomas during lunch. **But even though** someone pushed Mr. Thomas, causing his lunch tray to fall to the floor, the whole incident lasted only a few minutes. **And not a single student** was disciplined for anything that occurred in the lunchroom that day. Mr. Thomas even reacted to the lunchroom incident by simply ignoring the hecklers. **But even if** the lunchroom incident qualifies as some form of actual disruption, it was no more disruptive than what happened in *Tinker*. The Court in *Tinker* recognized that a student's free speech "does not end at the school door."
>
> **So, too, should this court.**

Example 2

Again, compare the before and after versions. This example uses traditional transitions and phrasing.

> The Government's reliance **on the case of** *Michigan v. Bryant* is distinguishable **based on the facts and circumstances. First**, that case was limited to the relationship between interrogation, hearsay, and the Confrontation Clause. **In contrast**, there was no interrogation in the case at bar. **Second**, Dr. Campbell's report was not created in response to an "ongoing emergency." **Moreover**, the Government's investigation and analysis deliberately targeted Stephenson with the goal of creating evidence that could positively identify him as the murderer at trial. **Third**, the fact that Dr. Campbell conducted her analysis in her own facility does not mean that the report was non-testimonial in nature. **It is important to note that** regardless of where the analysis was conducted, if a "statement is made under circumstances which would lead an objective witness reasonably to believe that the statement would be made available for use at a later trial," that statement is testimonial. *Crawford*, 541 U.S. at 52. **In conclusion**, the judgment of the trial court should be affirmed by this Court.

And this version uses lighter alternatives:

> The Government's reliance on *Michigan v. Bryant* **is simply misplaced** because that case was limited to the relationship between interrogation, hearsay, and the Confrontation Clause. Here, there was no interrogation. What's more, Dr. Campbell's report was not created in response to an "ongoing emergency." **Instead**, the Government's investigation and analysis deliberately targeted Stephenson with the goal of creating evidence that could positively identify him as the murderer. **Just because** Dr. Campbell conducted her analysis in her own

> facility does not mean that the report was non-testimonial. **That is so because** a statement is testimonial if made under circumstances which would lead an objective witness reasonably to believe that the statement would be made available for use at a later trial. **And that remains so** regardless of where the analysis was conducted. *Crawford*, 541 U.S. at 52. **At bottom,** the Government asks this court to allow the Government to approach an expert witness, provide her with images that were unlawfully obtained, and then task her with creating an image of a "perpetrator" for use at trial. **No court has ever extended *Bryant* this far. Nor should this Court.**

Example 3

The topic sentence for this paragraph is bogged down by the full citation and does not provide much useful information. The paragraph uses traditional transitions to enumerate.

> In *Comedy III Prods., Inc. v. Gary Saderup, Inc.*, 21 P.3d 797, 803 (Cal. 2001), the California Supreme Court said that the purpose of the First Amendment is two-fold. First, the First Amendment works to preserve an uninhibited marketplace of ideas in which individuals can create, devise, and invent without unnecessary limits. *Id.* Second, the First Amendment nurtures individual's self-expression by fostering individual growth and self-realization. *Id.* Courts have extended this right and protection to video games such as the one created by Mr. Crow. *See Hamilton v. Speight*, 827 F. App'x 238, 240 (3d Cir. 2020).

Notice this alternative gets the citation out of the way and gives the reader something useful and concise. In doing so, it also shortens the entire paragraph.

The First Amendment preserves an uninhibited marketplace of ideas and nurtures an individual's self-expression and growth. *Comedy III Prods., Inc. v. Gary Saderup, Inc.*, 21 P.3d 797, 803 (Cal. 2001); *see also Hamilton v. Speight*, 827 F. App'x 238, 240 (3d Cir. 2020).

And One More Thing

Simple tools like headings, subheadings, paragraph structure, and transitions turn your legal writing into legal thinking. Heading by heading, paragraph by paragraph, point by point. That creates cohesiveness. And cohesiveness separates a brief that readers can follow from a brief that simply contains words on the page.

CHAPTER XII

Making MORE Revisions: Clarity

A. Dead Bodies and Word Gravel

According to Wikipedia, legendary lawyer Gerry Spence has never lost a criminal trial and hasn't lost a civil case since 1969. Although he's now in his mid-90's and retired, you should put down this guide immediately and look him up. In the meantime, here's what he had to say about legal writing:

> When it comes to plain talk, lawyers are the worst. Most speak and write as if they live in a repository for dead bodies. When they write a brief that some poor trapped judge must read, they fill them with heavy, gray, lifeless, disgustingly boring word gravel—piles of it, tons of it. When I read most briefs, I want to scream. I want to throw the brief out the window and jump.[1]

That may not be a hot take, but it certainly is a grim one. He's not wrong. I've seen TONS of word gravel over the years, and I've shoveled more than my share into my own writing. What can we do?

---

[1] Gerry Spence, *How to Argue and Win Every Time* (1995).

You guessed it. More revisions, this time focusing on sentence clarity.

B. Sentence Structure

Do you remember being in middle school and learning how to diagram sentences? Well, forget all that. For one thing, your supervisor is rarely if ever going to ask you to diagram a sentence in a brief that must be filed in the next two hours. For another thing, you don't need a diagram to improve sentences.

When I give students a list of sentences to revise as an in-class exercise, they do so intuitively. The room gets quiet. They lock into what's on the page. They immediately make sentences more concise. They replace awkward phrases. They omit extra words. They even find better words. All without diagramming anything.

That's a bit like what you can do with a rough draft. Imagine every sentence is alone on the page. Don't let any sentence hide amongst a bunch of other long and awkward sentences that tumbled onto the page while you were still doing the research and reviewing the record. *That's* when you'll see the need for revisions. Here are some things to look for even when you're in a hurry.

1. Problems in Plain View

If the clock is really ticking, find the sentences that are three or more lines long. Don't be surprised if those sentences contain colons, semicolons, or phrases set off by commas. And don't be surprised if they are run on sentences. Long, complex sentences are common in a rough draft, and they nearly always need attention. So, look for those first.

2 More Problems in Plain View: Unnecessary Words and Phrases

There's a good chance that the long sentences you found in plain view had common phrases that don't add anything. Stop me if you've seen some of these. Ask yourself if they can be removed or replaced with a one-word alternative

- Applying the foregoing principles
- It is important to note that
- Because of the fact that
- Under the relevant facts and circumstances
- Unless and until
- At the present time
- On a number of occasions
- At that point in time
- In light of the fact that

You get the idea. In a rough draft, we often use extra words and phrases before getting to the point because we aren't sure what the point is. Or we use extra words out of habit because we had to satisfy some minimum page or word requirement in high school or college.

Either way, they can be omitted from your legal writing most of the time. For example, if something is truly "important to note," you can use that phrase once. But if everything is "important to note," then nothing is.

3 Problems in Hiding

a. Passive Voice

Passive voice occurs when the writer makes the object of an action into the subject of a sentence. (I had to look that up.) Earlier in the guide we recognized that passive voice can be helpful when used intentionally:

- Mistakes were made.
- Alcohol was consumed.
- Injuries were received by the plaintiff.
- An excessive dose of medication was prescribed.
- Records were misplaced.

But passive voice can be unhelpful when used unintentionally. It's not grammatically wrong. But it adds length to a sentence, which, in turn, affects clarity. Like these examples:

Passive: The verdict returned by the jury was not guilty.

Active: The jury returned a not guilty verdict.

Passive: The testimony given by the eyewitnesses stated that the victim was shot by the defendant.

Active: The eyewitnesses testified that the defendant shot the victim.

Passive: Mistakes were made when several associates were let go.

Active: Senior partners wrongfully fired several young associates.

Passive: The ruling by the trial judge was erroneous.

Active: The trial judge erred.

Passive: The trial court's ruling was that the testimony of the witness was admissible as non-hearsay.

Active: The trial judge ruled that the witness's testimony was non-hearsay.

b. Nominalizations

Nominalizations are nouns created with verbs or adjectives. That's an impressive way of saying "one word will do." As you read these, ask yourself what one word could have been used.

- The trial judge reached the conclusion that the jury should be sequestered.
- The defendant made the decision to go to trial.
- The court placed emphasis on the victim's testimony.
- The parties gave consideration to a settlement.
- The trial judge made a ruling in favor of the plaintiff.
- The attorney made an argument that the plaintiff was at fault.
- The parties reached a stipulation that expert testimony was relevant.
- The mediator helped in facilitating an agreement.
- The parties were in disagreement.
- The exhibits created confusion for the jury.
- The doctor's testimony was a distortion of the facts.
- The police refused to launch an investigation.

If you want to check your work, the words were concluded, decided, emphasized, considered, ruled, argued, stipulated, facilitated, disagreed, confused, distorted, and investigate.

You're welcome.

4. *Combining Problems*

You can get away with long sentences, extra words, passive voice, and nominalizations on occasion. In fact, I'm pretty sure I used passive voice or nominalizations several times in this guide just to see if you were paying attention. (Just kidding. I probably just missed them, like we all do.) But what happens when they are strung together? You guessed it. They create long sentences, three lines or more. Which takes us back to problems in plain view. Find the problems in the following sentences. Better yet, rewrite them.

- After reviewing the record and applying the key legal principles, it is clear that the trial court gave consideration to the arguments of both sides before making the suggestion that the parties should try to reach an agreement and arrive at a settlement.
- Because the case of *Miller v. Johnson* was overruled by the Supreme Court of Alabama, it is uncertain at the present time whether or not a violation of the fifth amendment occurred when officers made an arrest of the defendant and prosecutors later tried to introduce evidence of his post-arrest, pre-*Miranda* silence at trial.
- After due consideration of the present case, which includes the four elements set forth in the statute, the court should reach the conclusion that the sentence imposed on the defendant was unlawful; indeed, the sentence was cruel and unusual under the eighth amendment.

5. *Style*

After you get a handle on revising sentences for clarity, think about the choice of words. We learn a lot of legalese and formal terms in law school that sneak into our writing. Before law school, you never in your entire life "exited a vehicle." You simply "got out of a car."

You don't know a single person who would say: "Joe consumed two beers in the course of his commerce at Newby Brewery and, prior thereto, he had indulged in the consumption of at least two but no more than four more of the aforementioned beers at the Old Alliance Pub." You might say: "Joe drank two beers at Newby and three beers at Old Alliance."

(At which point you would add, hopefully, "Joe got a ride home.").

The lesson? Write like a reasonably normal person talks. A good way to gauge how your writing "sounds" is to read your brief out loud. You may feel ridiculous and annoy those around you. But hey, no one ever said legal writing was easy.

6. *Short Sentences*

In a brief with hundreds of sentences and thousands of words, short sentences add punch. Check these out.

- Congress was quick to respond.
- So too here.
- But the President had no authority to do so.
- That is the point.
- The facts were tragically simple.
- They were successful.
- Not so.

- The Plaintiff failed to do so.
- They were told to peddle their scare tactics elsewhere.

A good goal is for every paragraph to have one sentence that begins and ends on the same line. Every now and then—not too often—make a short sentence its very own paragraph.

That really pops.

7. Examples

Remember the in-class exercises I mentioned? Here's an entire list of examples for you to review. I've given the answers to the first few. Try the rest on your own.

1. It is important to note that the primary issue in the present case is whether or not damages may or may not be recovered by the plaintiff in this case.

   Better: The issue is whether the plaintiff may recover damages.

2. In light of the facts and circumstances in the case at bar, it appears that Ms. Johnson has a very strong case.

   Better: Ms. Johnson has a strong case.

3. In applying the foregoing principles to the case, we see that the case involving Ms. Johnson presents a similar situation as the plaintiff in *Miller*.

   Better: Ms. Johnson's case is like Miller's.

4. We would submit that several strong and compelling arguments have been raised by the plaintiff.

   Better: The plaintiff has several strong arguments.

5. The plaintiff made an argument that the Defendant's conduct was marked by fraud.

   Better: The plaintiff argued that the Defendant's conduct was fraudulent.

6. The court went on to place considerable emphasis on the importance of balancing the interest of the minor with the interest of the business.

7. The suspect was observed exiting his vehicle while in possession of a firearm; he was thereafter arrested by police officers who were of the opinion they possessed reasonable and articulate suspicion that criminal activity was being engaged in by the suspect.

8. In this case, this Court must apply the aforementioned landmark case of *Tinker* to the facts and circumstances of the case at bar.

9 It is important to note that the fact that Dr. Campbell conducted her analysis in her own facility does not mean that this court should make the finding that the report was non-testimonial in nature.

10. Although *Marsh* and *Galloway* together lay the framework for the legislative prayer test that both the Supreme Court and various district courts have applied for the past half-century, a more recent Fifth Circuit case, *Am. Humanist Ass'n v. McCarty*, has further expanded this test to likewise apply to school board prayer in holding that one public school board's policy of inviting students to pray before school-board meetings did not violate the Establishment Clause.

11. Where a defendant gives publicity to a matter relating to the private life of a plaintiff, this defendant is liable if the plaintiff shows only that it would be highly offensive to a reasonable person and is not of legitimate public concern.

12. The Plaintiff simply does not have the ability to meet such a burden, as he does not have affirmative proof that the purpose of the School Board for implementing this policy had anything to do with religion at all.

13. The overriding concerns which led the Court to the determination that the statutes in *Lemon* were unconstitutional orbited around the fact that the overall religiosity of the schools and instructors highly contributed to the effect of the statute.

14. The rice in the church, where there had been a wedding, was picked up by Eleanor Rigby.

15. The verdict returned by the jury revealed that the jury gave consideration to testimony presented by a defense expert.

16. The ruling of the trial judge indicated that great emphasis was placed on testimony of the victim.

17. It is important to note that the verdict returned by the jury revealed that the jury gave consideration to testimony presented by a defense expert.

18. The ruling of the trial judge against the defendant in this case indicated that great emphasis was placed on the testimony of the victim because of the fact the victim identified the defendant.

19. Because of the fact that he had the burden of proof, the plaintiff gave consideration to finding an expert who would give consideration to whether or not the doctor satisfied the aforementioned standard of care.

20. Under the facts and circumstances, it is important to note that the defendant failed to raise and assert the defense of self-defense.

C. Citation Sentences

Did you know there's now a 23rd edition of the Bluebook? It's true. Congratulations to the publishers and editors and good luck to the present and future law review members among you. But what does that mean for the rest of us?

The intricacies of legal citation for primary and secondary authority for federal courts and fifty states could easily overwhelm a concise guide to appellate advocacy (you know, such as this one). The very thought overwhelms me, I'll tell you that much. As all law students learn, the Bluebook contains the "blue pages," which consist of maybe sixty or so pages devoted to legal memoranda, court documents, and briefs; the white pages, which devote several hundred pages to academic writing; and a whole bunch of rules and tables.

Here's the good news. This is a practical guide meant for students and practitioners. We can mostly just follow the blue pages.[2] And for readers of this short and happy guide, here are a few more reminders and suggestions that highlight the importance of doing so.

---

[2] "Just follow the blue pages." Now *that's* some quality instruction. No need to thank me. You're more than welcome.

1. Professionalism and Credibility

Remember your roadmaps and case examples? Legal citations show the reader where those legal principles and examples are found. If the reader—if a judge—relies on a citation in your brief and does not find that principle or that example, the credibility of your entire argument crumbles. Even if an error resulted from a mistyped or transposed number. And *especially* if the error was the fevered dream of some AI platform.

2. Consistency

I should probably put this next section in a footnote or maybe whisper so we don't get in trouble. But this is based on my observations and experiences, so here goes: all a court really wants and expects is accurate citations to cases and statutes. They generally won't get hung up on which words to abbreviate and capitalize, and they may not know the latest way to cite an internet law review. They might. And a partner you're working with might, too. So, do everything you can to be bluebook compliant in the time that you have.

But.

Regardless of the technical requirement, be consistent with yourself throughout the brief. Let's say you have a full cite to this case: *McIntyre v. Balentine*, 833 S.W.2d 52 (Tenn. 1992).

A short citation may look like this: *McIntyre,* 833 S.W.2d at 55.

But a few pages later in the brief, it should not suddenly be *McIntyre*, at 55. Nor should it be <u>McIntrye</u>, 833 S.W.2d at 55. Nor should it be *McIntyre v. Balentine,* 833 S.W.2d at 55. And it most definitely should not be *Balentine*, 833 S.W.2d at 55. That would be several different citations for the same source that can't all be correct. Moreover, the reader would learn (a) that you weren't sure which one was correct, (b) that you didn't care which one was correct, (c) that you didn't notice the problem, or (d) that you were running out of time.

Likewise, let's say you cite this statute: Tenn. Code Ann. § 39-13-202(a), It should not be cited elsewhere in the brief as T.C.A. § 39-13-202(a). You should, of course, check to see which one is correct. But if you don't, at least pick one and stick with it.

Make sense? These errors don't only look like bluebook errors. They look like proofreading errors. And that's two strikes against you.

3. Quotations

Be especially attentive to the rules on quotations, particularly when altering a quote or omitting material from the quote. Any ideas or examples in a brief that are not yours must be attributed to a source. And if the exact language is used, it must be quoted. Simple idea, right?

You'd be surprised how often this is done wrong or not done at all. A quote shows that you have used the exact language found in a court decision or statute. If you alter that language, even accidentally, the court may think you're misrepresenting the law. Yikes. Therefore, use an ellipsis in the middle or at the end of a quotation to tell a reader material has been left out intentionally. Again, there are specific rules and examples in the Bluebook and other citation sources to make sure you get this right. The point here is that your attention to detail polishes your work product and enhances your credibility and professionalism.

4. Style

We talked about this earlier but just a quick reminder. One way to write a concise sentence is to remove clutter. Few things create clutter quite like a citation to a case or statute in the beginning or middle of a sentence. Think about putting the full citation at the end of the sentence Compare these before and after examples:

- In *McIntrye v. Balentine*, 833 S.W.2d 52 (Tenn. 1992), the Tennessee Supreme Court adopted a system of modified comparative fault to allow plaintiffs to recover if their degree of negligence does not exceed that of the defendant.
- A system of modified comparative fault to allow plaintiffs to recover if their degree of negligence does not exceed that of the defendant. *McIntrye v. Balentine*, 833 S.W.2d 52 (Tenn. 1992).
- Tennessee Code Annotated section 39-13-202 states that first-degree murder requires evidence that a defendant acted with intent and premeditation.
- First degree murder requires evidence that a defendant acted with intent and premeditation. Tenn. Code Ann. § 39-13-202.
- In the leading cases of *Apprendi v. New Jersey*, 530 U.S. 466 (2000), *Blakely v. Washington*, 542 U.S. 296 (2004), *and United States v. Booker*, 543 U.S. 220 (2005), the United States Supreme Court ruled that the Sixth Amendment right to a jury trial requires that facts used to enhance a defendant's sentence above the statutory maximum for an offense must be found by a jury beyond a reasonable doubt.
- The Sixth Amendment right to a jury trial requires that facts used to enhance a defendant's sentence above the statutory maximum for an offense must be found by a jury beyond a reasonable doubt. *Apprendi*

v. New Jersey, 530 U.S. 466 (2000), *Blakely v. Washington*, 542 U.S. 296 (2004), *and United States v. Booker*, 543 U.S. 220 (2005)

And One More Thing

So now you have a plan for making your legal writing as clear as possible. But you still need time. These bright-line suggestions should help you revise every sentence. With practice, you will get more efficient at seeing them on the page. Until then, keep these two modest goals in mind: (1) If you are pressed for time, find and revise the longest sentence in each paragraph; and (2) If you are *really* pressed for time, just try to catch the longest sentence on each page.

Even small revisions will go a long way.

CHAPTER XIII

Oral Arguments

Oral argument before the panel of judges who will decide the outcome is often an important piece of appellate advocacy. *How* important can be a matter of opinion. Some courts always allow oral arguments, some rarely do, and others do upon request. Some judges are engaged in the oral argument; others look bored; others look agitated.

I've heard it said that a great oral argument will not rescue a poor brief. I tend to agree, which is why most of this guide talks about brief writing. But an oral argument is your only chance to engage in a conversation with the court, point out your strongest arguments, and address the court's questions and concerns. And when the court takes its next break, it often talks about your case as a panel for the first time. The big question is how to make the most of the opportunity.

A. Prepare Early

1. *Writing the Brief*

Start thinking about oral arguments when you're writing the brief. Think about what happens during an oral argument. You have a few minutes to tell the court the three "R's": result, roadmaps, and reasons. The good news is that the brief already did those things.

a. The Statement of the Issues

You know the court is going to ask about the issues. A judge, especially one who hasn't read the brief in advance, may even ask, "Counsel, what's the issue in this case?" When that moment comes, you will be glad your brief combined a legal principle and legally relevant facts as clearly and concisely as possible. You'll be thrilled that you devoted a lot of time to this specific task. You might even allow yourself a fist pump (in your mind, not in court). If nothing else, you'll avoid this scenario:

Court: Counsel, what exactly is the issue?

Counsel: The issue is whether the trial court erred.

Court: Can you be more specific?

Counsel: Whether the trial court erred in this case.

Court: (*Closes eyes, rubs temples.*)

b. Summary of the Argument

You have very little time to convey the importance of your case and tell the court your strongest arguments.

Tick tock.

Guess where you already did that? The summary of the argument is a great place to find your overall theme and an outline of your main points for oral argument.

c. Point Headings and CREACS

Remember when we talked about putting the point headings and subheadings of the argument in the table of contents, all in one place? If that was done correctly, you created an outline that will guide your oral argument through the *result* you want, the *roadmap*, and the *reasons*. If that was *not* done correctly, you'll likely struggle to put the pieces together while standing before an appellate panel for fifteen minutes.

2. Anticipate Questions

As you begin your argument, one of the judges on the panel will interrupt and ask questions. They want to determine whether your arguments hold up under scrutiny. Moreover, they want to find the weaknesses in your arguments.

Knowing that, wouldn't it be great to find the weaknesses in your argument well in advance of oral argument and address them in your brief? Here's a pro tip: the weaknesses are hiding in the areas where the brief was hardest to write. Rather than waiting for lightning to strike during oral argument, make time to practice or "moot" your arguments out loud (or to yourself) *as you are working on the brief.*

Arrange a practice oral argument about a week *before* the brief is due. Have someone ask about the record, the case law, the statutes, the arguments, and anything else. That's how you'll find the weaknesses in your argument *while there's still time to address them in the brief.* If you do these things, you will be more than prepared for whatever's next.

B. Formal Oral Argument

If an oral argument were held ten times, my guess is it would seem like ten different experiences. The judges on the panel may be active or passive. The lawyers arguing the case have good days and bad days. Some days are sharper than others. And quite simply, there are some things you can control and some you can't.

1. Things You Control

a. Preparation

Like anything else, the earlier you prepare the better. Find out how much time a court allows each side for oral arguments. If you're the appellant, prepare as though you will leave some of that time for rebuttal. If possible, watch other oral arguments in that court; many are live streamed or maintained on the court's website.

In addition, be sure to do the following tasks.

- Review the record. Even if you were not the trial attorney, the court expects you to be an expert on what's in the record.
- Review the briefs.
- Update the research. Don't be caught off guard when the court brings up some very recent decision or amended statute.
- Update the research cited by the opposing party and the lower courts.
- As discussed earlier, think about how portions of the brief may be viewed through a lens of oral argument.
- Practice out loud. In the office. At home for your spouse. In your car. In the shower. On the phone with your mom. You will get used to hearing your voice

and you will develop some muscle memory for phrasing.

b. Appearance

This is easy. Judges wear robes, lawyers wear suits. Navy blue or gray. Take your pick. As someone once said, you are a member of the bar, so make sure your clothes don't suggest you've wandered into the *wrong* bar.

c. Presentation

Just like the brief, your oral argument must tell the court *what* result you want, *how* it can reach that result, and *why* it should reach that result. But in oral argument, you must do these things in fifteen or twenty minutes.

Remember several chapters ago we talked about identifying the issues for appeal, assessing the strength of those issues, and thinking about the order in which to present them?

Good, because that applies here, too.

You may have one good issue or ten good issues. But you can only start with one, and you will have time for only a few. Assess the issues based on the same factors: updated research, the standard of review, and the presence of reversible error (or harmless error if you're the appellee).

d. Delivery

i. Appellant

Wait for the case to be called, stand up, and walk to the podium. Take as little with you as possible. Some take a legal pad with an outline. Some write notes on a manilla folder. Some brave souls take nothing. I do not recommend taking a laptop, tablet, or phone. The more you take the more you will look down (at best), read (not great), and fumble (at worst).

At the podium, begin with, "May it Please the Court." Why must it please the Court? I don't know, it just does. Introduce yourself and identify the party you represent. If you are the appellant, reserve a few minutes for rebuttal. If you're going to present a factual overview, keep it concise. Lawyers often get bogged down in the facts before they even get to the issues. Tell the court the issue you intend to discuss, and the relief sought. Do this as a conclusion:

> "Respectfully, Your Honors, the trial court abused its discretion in allowing a chiropractor called by the plaintiff to testify about the standard of care applicable to an orthopedist."

Not,

> "The first issue we intend to argue is whether or not the trial court erred in allowing a chiropractor to testify about the standard of care applicable to an orthopedist. It's our position that the trial court erred and that the error was an abuse of discretion."

If you're going to argue more than one issue, state all three conclusions and then transition with something like, "Turning to our first issue, Your Honors." That way you made time to state all three conclusions even if you don't have enough time to argue all of them. And you likely won't. Follow the CREAC approach for each issue:

The conclusion.

The legal principles and framework.

A similar case you want the court to follow.

The application of those principles to the facts of your case.

Conclude by telling the court the result you want. If you run out of time in mid-sentence, ask the court for permission to finish your sentence. And then conclude that sentence.

ii. Appellee

Before you take the podium, listen carefully to the appellant's arguments and the court's questions. You already have several advantages:

- You're defending the status quo.
- You get to hear what the appellant has to say. You get to hear what's on the court's mind.

When the appellant concludes, walk to the podium and say, "May it Please the Court." Introduce yourself. Now it's time to deploy your advantage. Rather than turn to the roadmap and preplanned points you had in mind, be flexible.

- You might begin with the issue the court focused on during your opponent's argument.
- You might answer a question that was posed to your opponent, particularly if your opponent struggled with it.
- You might clarify the authority or the record, particularly if the opponent misstated something.

Once you capitalize on those opportunities, turn to the points you had planned to make. Follow the roadmap outlined above for the appellant.

2. Things You Don't Control

An active panel of judges will ask questions. The questions tend to fit into two categories: the ones you can predict and the ones you maybe can't.

a. Predictable Questions

i Is That in the Record, Counsel?

Even if you did not represent the client at trial, you must know the answers to questions about the record. "Yes, Your Honor. An offer of proof was made during a jury out hearing at trial." If you can't recall, just say so. Do not guess. And do NOT tell the court you don't know what's in the record because you did not try the case. They HATE that. (Yes, I just went all caps on you.) And that harms your credibility.

ii. What Rule Are You Asking Us to Apply?

Well, that's easy enough, right? That's what the "R" in the CREAC was all about.

- "Section 101 has three elements, Your Honor. In our case only the third is at issue."
- "The court has always applied a two-prong test, Your Honor, and the evidence fails to establish either in this case."
- "This court has never addressed this particular issue, so we urge the court to adopt the approach followed by the majority of jurisdictions."

iii. What's the Standard of Review?

Again, this is something you must know about each issue. And it's a required component of the brief.

iv. What Have Other Courts Done?

Sounds like the "E" in the CREAC. Be concise. Remember we talked about the perils of getting bogged down when summarizing and applying prior cases in the brief. Just imagine how that sounds out loud. Therefore, if you worked on writing concise paragraphs about case law in your brief, you will be ready to discuss them during the oral argument. That said, remember, the court is likely going to ask you about cases the opposing side relies on. Spend time preparing to distinguish those cases in advance and you'll be glad the court asked.

v. What Did the Lower Court Do Wrong?

Sounds like the "A" in the CREAC. Remember when we talked about how transitions can enumerate your key points in the brief? Oral argument is another great time to break out the "first, second, and finally" technique. Few things are more impressive than the ability to listen to a question, respond by saying something like, "Two points, Your Honor," and then confidently making two points. That's more than making an argument; that's taking command of the material and educating everyone in the room.

vi. What Relief Are You Seeking?

Sounds like the "C" in the CREAC. Remember to assert why an error either does or does not merit relief.

b. Hypothetically Speaking

If you have prepared with these ideas in mind, you will be ready to answer questions about what's in record, what's in your brief, what's in the opposing brief, what the lower court did wrong (appellants), and what the court did right (appellees).

But how do you answer questions you didn't think of before the argument. Something the judge has imagined? Something that's entirely hypothetical? This happens a lot, particularly with a question of first impression or a case before a law development court.

Here's the good news about hypothetical questions. You can't really be wrong when you answer them. I mean, who really knows with absolute certainty the answer to something that's truly hypothetical? The key is to *try* to answer the question. The only wrong answer is this: "That's not what we have in this case, Your Honors." They know that. They are asking you to assume a point.

More good news? These are opportunities. In a close case, you and the opponent kick the ball around a bit. But the lawyer who knows how the legal principles really work—how they apply to your case and future cases—gains the advantage. If you worked your way through this guide and others, if you preserved viable issues, if you did the research, if you constructed CREACS (or other devices), if you really thought about *why* the court should rule in your favor, you will advocate *and* educate. That's what the best advocates do.

Still more good news? If you miss a hypothetical or two, it's not the end of the world. It's entirely possible the hypothetical questions made no sense to anyone other than the judge who posed the question. Do your best and then move on. Remember the brief will usually matter more than one missed question at oral argument.

And One More Thing

More than one judge has said that "you have X number of minutes, but you're not required to use them all." Conclude when you have made your key points and requested relief. If you run out of time in mid-sentence, stop and ask the court for permission to conclude your answer. And then stop.

Full stop.

CHAPTER XIV

Future

In the coming years, the landscape of appellate advocacy is poised to undergo transformative shifts driven by technological advancements and evolving legal norms. Technology will enable more accessible and efficient appellate processes, with virtual hearings becoming commonplace, facilitating broader participation and reducing logistical barriers. Artificial intelligence and data analytics will revolutionize legal research, empowering advocates with predictive tools to anticipate judicial reasoning and refine arguments. Furthermore, the integration of multimedia presentations and interactive visual aids will enhance the persuasive impact of appellate arguments, fostering clearer and more compelling storytelling in the courtroom. As legal frameworks adapt to societal changes, appellate advocacy will increasingly prioritize issues at the intersection of technology, ethics, and human rights, shaping a future where innovation and tradition converge to redefine the standards of persuasive legal discourse.

Guess what?

The preceding paragraph was created when I asked ChatGPT to discuss the future of appellate advocacy. I can't disagree with those observations. I'm not even sure I understand them. I do know they don't sound like me. Let's take a closer look.

ChatGPT: In the coming years, the landscape of appellate advocacy is poised to undergo transformative shifts driven by technological advancements and evolving legal norms.

Me: Technology will change appellate advocacy.

ChatGPT: Technology will enable more accessible and efficient appellate processes, with virtual hearings becoming commonplace, facilitating broader participation and reducing logistical barriers.

Me: Technological advances will reduce barriers and increase participation.

ChatGPT: Artificial intelligence and data analytics will revolutionize legal research, empowering advocates with predictive tools to anticipate judicial reasoning and refine arguments.

Me: Let's hope so.

ChatGPT: Furthermore, the integration of multimedia presentations and interactive visual aids will enhance the persuasive impact of appellate arguments, fostering clearer and more compelling storytelling in the courtroom.

Me: Sure, as long as the presentations, visual aids, and stories are based on what's properly in the appellate record. (You knew I'd say that at least one more time in this guide.)

ChatGPT: As legal frameworks adapt to societal changes, appellate advocacy will increasingly prioritize issues at the intersection of technology, ethics, and human rights, shaping a future where innovation and tradition converge to redefine the standards of persuasive legal discourse.

Me: Huh?

Style considerations aside, ChatGPT's point about advances in technology is undeniable. To some extent, that's not new. In the last three or four decades the practice of law evolved from typewriters to word processors to word documents to computerized research to email to electronic filing. At the time, many of these developments felt like landing on the moon.

By comparison, technological advances in recent years have felt like landing on Mars. Artificial intelligence platforms for research, analysis, and legal writing have transformed the practice of law.[1] These tools can do research, write briefs, and analyze points of law. They can save time and money and increase access to justice. They can also get lawyers in big trouble. We have all heard about lawyers who submitted briefs containing "authority" that some AI platform took the liberty of hallucinating.[2] (And consider that "hallucinated" is a euphemism for "misrepresented" or "lied.") If that doesn't strike fear into the heart of every lawyer, then I don't know what to tell you. Legal education and the practice of law will have to adapt in ways that exceed the scope (and pace) of this *Short and Happy Guide*.[3]

---

[1] *See generally* Eugene Volokh, *Chief Justice Robots*, 68 Duke L.J.1135 (2019) (discussing the various roles for artificial intelligence in legal practice, including writing briefs).

[2] Speaking of which, check this out. A recent empirical study found that two leading legal research tools hallucinated results 17% to 32% of the time. Varun Magesh et al., *Hallucination Free? Assessing the Reliability of Leading Legal Research Tools*, Journal of Empirical Legal Studies (2025 0:1-27).

[3] Dessislave Dobrev, *The Human Lawyer in the Age of Artificial Intelligence: Doomed for Extinction or in Need of a Survival Manual*, 18 J. Int'l Bus. & L. 39, 40 (2018) (arguing that law schools should "devise wholly new curricula to equip lawyers with the skills to compete in an AI future").

So let's end this guide where we began. If you love a good challenge and you *really* love legal research and writing, appellate advocacy may be for you. The ideas and methods in this guide will get you started and allow you to grow. You will represent clients with competence and diligence. And you will overcome procedural obstacles, analyze legal issues, and write with cohesiveness and clarity.

And there's more.

With experience, you will develop a reputation for excellence in this unique area. You will become the expert at your law firm or agency. You will be the person others turn to when a case takes a bad turn or a client is handed an unfavorable verdict or ruling. You may be involved in cases that become controlling authority and shape the law for generations to come. Above all, you will be able to serve with professionalism and excellence regardless of the outcome. The path won't always be Short or Happy, but success will follow.

I wish you all the best!